necessary.

by Zenja Glass

Copyright© 2023 by Zenja Glass

First Edition.

This publication is written to give hope and inspiration to others. It is sold with the understanding that the author and publisher is not engaged in giving psychological, legal, nor financial, or other professional advice. Please seek the services of a qualified professional if expert counseling is needed. The author disclaims any liability incurred from using or applying any information contained in this book. This book is intended for age 18 and older.

Scripture quotations marked (NIV) are taken from The Holy Bible, New International Version®, NIV®. Copyright © 1973, 1978, 1984, 2011 by Biblica, Inc.™ Used by permission of Zondervan. All rights reserved worldwide. www.zondervan.com The "NIV" and "New International Version® are trademarks registered in the United States Patent and Trademark Office by Biblica, Inc.™

Scripture quotations marked (KJV) are taken from the King James Version (KJV) of the Bible, public domain.

Scripture quotations marked (ESV) are taken from the ESV® Bible (The Holy Bible, English Standard Version®), copyright © 2001 by Crossway, a publishing ministry of Good News Publishers. Used by permission. All rights reserved. The ESV text may not be quoted in any publication made available to the public by a Creative Commons license. The ESV may not be translated in whole or in part into any other language.

Scripture quotations marked (NASB) are taken from the (NASB®) New American Standard Bible®, Copyright© 1960, 1971, 1977, 1995, 2020 by The Lockman Foundation. Used by permission. All rights reserved. www.lockman.org

No part of this publication may be reproduced, sold, stored in retrieval systems, reposted, uploaded, scanned, recorded, or distributed in any manner, or in any form, including as a book, eBook, audible recording, video, etc., without permission from Zenja Glass. Violating this request is considered as theft of intellectual property. For permission to use any material from this book, or to use any audio or video footage, please visit: www.ZenjaGlass.com to submit your request.

ISBN: 979-8-218-13790-8 (print), 979-8-218-18924-2 (audio)

Printed in the United States of America

I lay myself naked before the world to help the brokenhearted find hope in God.

I am already dead.

Dead to myself.

Alive in Christ!

by Zenja Glass

Contents

1. A Letter to the Enemy - Part 1 — 8
2. Head of Household — 18
3. Through the Fire — 28
4. Seek God First? — 46
5. The Pruning Season — 62
6. Strange Favor — 72
7. God Can Do More with Less — 84
8. Is It Mine? — 96
9. Open Your Eyes! — 110
10. Hidden — 120
11. The Secret Place — 132
12. Caged Mindset — 144
13. Letting Go — 154
14. I Won't Apologize for Going Higher! — 168
15. The Price of Elevation — 178
16. Thank Your Naysayers! — 192
17. REST — 200
18. Horseback Ride — 212
19. You Are a Lion! — 222
20. If Greatness Could Speak — 232
21. If I Were Your Enemy! — 242
22. When God Says No! — 252
23. Chapter Twenty-Three — 262
24. A Letter to the Enemy - Part 2 — 272

Dedication — 279

Afterword — 283

Acknowledgements — 288

About the Author — 290

[Audio/Video version of this book is available at ZenjaGlass.com]

[Audio/Video version of this book is available at ZenjaGlass.com]

Chapter 1

Affirmation – A Letter to the Enemy - Part 1

You tried to destroy me because you saw something in me

That I did not see in myself.

And you almost succeeded.

But I serve an almighty God who saw the best in me,

Even when I was at my lowest point in life.

My Father has exposed your lies!

And I no longer believe your version of who I am.

I am a child of the King of kings!

I am an heir of God!

[Audio/Video version of this book is available at ZenjaGlass.com]

Chapter 1

A Letter to the Enemy - Part 1

Did you really think you had free will to do whatever you pleased in my life?

You were being played like a puppet all along because you failed to notice your strings. Had you taken the time to simply look up, you would have realized my Father always kept a watchful eye over me. You never had free reign to rule in my life! And you never had the power to determine my destiny!

When I listened to your lying tongue, it sounded like the truth. My goodness! It sounded like the truth, and no one could convince me otherwise. You played your role so well that you almost succeeded in making me doubt myself. You almost succeeded in making me give up. You almost convinced me that while I was in the deepest valleys, my Father neither heard my many cries and prayers, nor cared to answer me because I wasn't worthy of His love and blessings.

You left me on my knees feeling unloved, used, angry, abandoned, confused, hurt, and sobbing in pain and grief. You whispered to me that my life would never get any better. You tried to convince me that God couldn't use me because I wasn't good enough. And though I wouldn't admit it, for a moment, I think I believed you.

But now I must say to you, your greatest mistake was not all the pain and sorrow you caused me.

necessary.

Your greatest mistake was leaving me on my knees... in the presence of my Father!

That's where you really messed up!

In your arrogance, you forgot who was my Overseer. As you celebrated the roles you played during some of the worst seasons of my life, you forgot who knew the ending before the beginning! Somehow, you failed to notice—before the curtains were opened, before your scenes began, before you played your wicked, evil role in my life—I was already predestined for greatness!

You messed up when you left me on my knees feeling insecure, fearful, weak, alone, unsure of who I was, and doubting my gifts and talents. It was in those painful, lonely seasons that I began to sit in the presence of my Father and recognize His voice and words of wisdom. He whispers! I guess I never sat long enough to realize... He actually whispers to me. I had no idea I could be strong in my weakest moments because His power is made perfect in weakness (2 Corinthians 12:9). I had no idea I could grow from dark places because He commands His angels concerning me (Psalm 91:11-12). And I had no idea it was possible to have great peace in the middle of my storms because God is able to give me peace that surpasses all understanding (Philippians 4:6-7).

So I thank you for leaving me on my knees, because without your help I never would have sat still long enough to discover that all along, my Father was trying to speak to me.

What is this that I now see?

My Father has exposed you!

What is this that I now see? I see strings! I see strings!

As I look up from my knees toward my Father in heaven, I now see... your strings are showing! You have been exposed!

A Letter to the Enemy - Part 1

Perhaps you should have paid closer attention to the conversation you had with my Father in the book of Job chapters one and two when your boundaries were set as you attacked Job's life. You are limited! You do not get a backstage pass to do whatever you wish to do in my life because my Overseer is always at work. And you cannot climb up your strings to take His place!

While you told many false lies, you failed to mention that God did not have to get off His throne to remove you from your place because you are NOT His equal! Archangel Michael and his angels fought against you, but you were not strong enough! They hurled you down to a small rock that we call earth (Revelation 12:7-9). You failed to mention that when God's children resist you, you must flee from us (James 4:7). You failed to mention the power and authority our Father has over you and how you begged Jesus again and again not to send you away (Mark 5:1-13). You failed to mention how you were driven out on several occasions and had no power over God (Matthew 8:16, Mark 1:39, Luke 4:31-35). And you certainly failed to mention that the same Spirit that raised Jesus Christ [Yeshua] from the dead now lives in us (Romans 8:11) and we are called to do even GREATER things (John 14:12-14)!

Interesting, isn't it? Many people say the greatest trick you have performed is by convincing the world that you don't exist. I think the greatest trick you have performed is by keeping us distracted with pain or pleasures so that we don't discover who we really are in the sight of God.

Now I see why you don't want us being still in His presence. I see why you love it when we don't have time to pray or to worship God. I see why you love to cause confusion and fighting among us. And I see why you love to keep our minds occupied with fruitless activities. Because if God's people truly understand the power that resides in us, and if our eyes are opened to the true

necessary.

spiritual battles, you would have no power! You would have no victories to call your own.

If only the world knew how limited you are!

If only the world truly knew that YOU are the one who fears the power of God at work in our lives!

Your confidence caused you to overlook the benefits of leaving me in a desolate land because it was in that barren place that I looked up and noticed your strings. You are indeed attached by strings with limitations. I shall no longer give ear to your lies or live in fear of your limited power. I am a child of the Highest King! I am an heir of God (Romans 8:16-17, Galatians 3:29, Galatians 4:6-7, Ephesians 3:6)! His power resides in me, and I in Him!

In your craftiness you caused me severe pain and sorrow, but I have come forth as pure gold in the sight of my Father. He knows He can trust me with pain... and blessings! He has wiped my tears away and He holds me with the right hand of His righteousness (Isaiah 41:10). The Lord is my fortress. Under His wings I find refuge and He covers me with His feathers (Psalm 91:2-4). He teaches me not to fear you because He has whispered to me, "The one who is in you is greater than the one who is in the world" (1 John 4:4 NIV).

So, while it may seem odd to say this, I thank you for the thorns you placed in my paths because they led me to new routes that glorified God and brought love, power, and purpose to my life! It was only when I was forced to stand alone, that I came to realize my Father never left my side. It was only when I couldn't see how I was going to make it, that I realized God was able to do so much more with less. It was only when I was too weak to stand, that I realized God was my strength, an ever-present help in times of trouble (Psalm 46:1). And it was only when I sat in the presence of my Father, feeling completely defeated, that I learned, "I can do all things through Christ which strengtheneth me" (Philippians 4:13 KJV).

I must end by saying, I am amazed by your acting skills. You are brilliant at distorting reality and trying to dominate center stage when it's your turn to act. And because God loves us enough to give us all free will, you seem to enjoy using some people to hurt others during your temporary confinement on this little rock.

I stand with my Father in the upper room and the curtains have been pulled back. Now I can clearly see that, all along, you were just a puppet with tricks and illusions, wreaking havoc in my life and playing your role in a scene that was already predestined for greatness (Ephesians 1:5, Jeremiah 1:5).

You preyed on my weaknesses and fears to the point where you almost had me. You almost succeeded in making me believe God was not present in my life and there was no hope of things ever getting better. You are a great liar! The father of lies (John 8:44)! And I almost believed you.

So I say to you, "Congratulations on a job well done! You delivered an Oscar-winning performance!"

Thank you for leaving me on my knees... in the presence of my Father!

Because now... I can see your strings!

Thank God Almighty... I can see your strings!

Reflection:

For so many years, I thought Satan had the power to do whatever he wanted to do in my life. I had no idea of his limitations, nor of

necessary.

the power that lived inside of me. I had no idea what it truly meant to walk in authority as a co-heir with Christ (Romans 8:17). And I certainly had no idea God's divine power was always at work in my life, even when I didn't feel His presence.

The enemy does not want us to look up toward our Father in heaven because he does not want us to know who stands above our circumstances! He does not have control to stop the power of God at work in our lives, so he operates with tricks and fearful illusions to try to get us to stop ourselves.

We must realize the enemy is limited. And he never wants us to notice his strings!

Recommended Reading:
- *The Spirit himself testifies with our spirit that we are God's children. Now if we are children, then we are heirs- heirs of God and co-heirs with Christ* (Romans 8:16-17 NIV).
- *Finally, be strong in the Lord and in his mighty power. Put on the full armor of God so that you can take your stand against the devil's schemes. For our struggle is not against flesh and blood, but against the rulers, against the authorities, against the powers of this dark world and against the spiritual forces of evil in the heavenly realms. Therefore put on the full armor of God, so that when the day of evil comes, you may be able to stand your ground, and after you have done everything, to stand* (Ephesians 6:10-13 NIV).
- *For he will command his angels concerning you to guard you in all your ways; they will lift you up in their hands, so that you will not strike your foot against a stone. You will*

A Letter to the Enemy - Part 1

tread upon the lion and the cobra; you will trample the great lion and the serpent. 'Because he loves me,' says the Lord, 'I will rescue him; I will protect him, for he acknowledges my name. He will call upon me, and I will answer him; I will be with him in trouble, I will deliver him and honor him. With long life I will satisfy him and show him my salvation (Psalm 91:11-16 NIV).

Assignment:

1. Are there any areas in your life where you are tempted to believe lies from the enemy? If so, what are they?

2. Write what each passage from the recommended reading means to you. Then ask yourself how you can implement this level of faith in your life on a daily basis.

[Audio/Video version of this book is available at ZenjaGlass.com]

Chapter 2

Affirmation – Head of Household

You'd better think twice before you go against a child of God.

Because when you attack me, you attack my Father!

And I don't ever recall Him losing a battle!

Don't be fooled by my outward appearance.

That is not where my true strength lies.

Look closer.

When you close your eyes and look closer,

You will be surprised to see

The army of God encamps all around me

With chariots of horses and fire!

My Father has never lost a battle.

And He never will!

[Audio/Video version of this book is available at ZenjaGlass.com]

Chapter 2

Head of Household

I will never forget the horrifying night my mother fled from an abusive relationship in the middle of the night with me and my young siblings.

She'd had enough.

And though I was only 12 years old, so had I.

I had witnessed many nights of drunken surprises, countless fights and abuse, but this time something was different. Things were taken to unimaginable levels. Without any warning, he lunged at my mother with an ice pick in his hand. He missed her head by just a few inches as she held my youngest sibling while doing her best to dodge him and scream for us to run out the front door. Somehow, he found out she was planning on leaving him. I couldn't help but wonder if he discovered the partially filled suitcases my mother was secretly packing away in my bedroom closet so that at the right time, when she was courageous enough, we would sneak away when he was at work, and never return again. He wasn't about to let that happen! And this time it wasn't just her life, but all our lives were in tremendous danger. It was the first time I wasn't sure if I would ever see my mother alive again.

So there we were, running down the street in the middle of the night, screaming for anyone to help us... looking for a savior. We found ourselves in the back of a neighbor's yard, running around their truck, pleading for them to call the police to save our lives.

necessary.

Little did I know I was running on a direct path right into the arms of God.

I distinctly remember the police picking us up in the middle of the night and driving us to the Greyhound bus station. My mother walked up to the man behind the counter and asked him, "Where is the next bus going?" He said, "Milwaukee, Wisconsin." She replied, "Then that's where we are going!" She had just enough money to buy our bus tickets, and I don't even recall if any of us were wearing shoes. It didn't matter. We were finally... free.

So there we were, my mother and myself, along with my two younger siblings, getting off the bus in downtown Milwaukee, Wisconsin, standing outside the bus station with no money, no plan, no home, and no support from anyone.

I will never forget the moment I heard my mother asking a stranger for a quarter so she could make a phone call. I remember thinking, "We don't even have a quarter? What are we going to do?"

But my mother was a praying woman, and despite our circumstances, she saw God in everything. She would always say God can make a way out of no way. Her faith in God was so strong, it somehow gave me comfort in the middle of our storm.

By sheer grace, God provided shelter for us a few nights through a distant relative; and within days, God opened doors for my mother to get on public assistance and get an apartment. She immediately enrolled in college and began her 10-year journey to receive a bachelor's degree and become a social worker.

The battle of abuse was finally over.

So, I thought.

Within months of fleeing to a new state, a new man entered our lives. I didn't like his fishy eyes the moment I met him. I saw the same demon in his eyes that we had just left behind. Only this time, I was watchful and ready to protect my family... at the ripe age of 12.

It was the middle of the night. I heard commotion in my mom's room. He was yelling at her for being on the phone and accusing her of talking with another man. Just as I turned the corner to make my presence known, I saw him hit my young mother so hard and with such a mighty force, it knocked her off the bed onto the floor and the phone completely shattered.

I stood there staring at that demon standing above my mother as though he'd taken his rightful place to ascend his throne.

A lion took over my small 90-pound frail body and I stood up to that beast with a power and a force that only came from my Father in heaven.

I reached into our kitchen drawer and grabbed a long silver blade with a huge handle that was almost too big for me to hold with one hand. I stood in the doorway, staring that beast off his throne as my mother begged me to go back to my room.

I didn't hear her.

I heard the thunder of clouds, the feet of armies by my side, and the thrust of 10,000 angels standing all around me. I stood in that doorway, legs spread apart and a blade in my left hand... ready for battle.

Time was frozen.

And I was unwilling to relent.

Unwilling to relive my past childhood trauma of witnessing countless episodes of abuse from demons on assignments.

He was a strong man with chocolate skin and red, beady eyes. I could tell from his brute, grim expression that he'd overtaken

necessary.

territories in the past. And I could sense he thought he'd conquered another one.

But this time he met his match!

He met his match in the body of a young 12-year-old girl with nations rising up inside of her.

I can still recall his heavy breathing. Fist still tightened. My mother was still on the floor, holding her bleeding mouth in agony.

But there she stood. A 90-pound warrior in pajamas, with a blade in her left hand, nearly too big to grip.

I courageously made a loud proclamation, "We will not go through this again! We did not come all this way to deal with the same stuff! GET OUT!!!"

He grinned. Then he laughed... nervously.

I stood there, as though having an out-of-body experience, watching myself... a young warrior refusing to surrender.

She did not take her eyes off her prey. She wasn't intimidated at all by his statue, nor his throne. She had nations rising up inside of her. That night, she was not only as bold as a lion... she became a lion!

She was frozen in time, standing in the doorway, legs spread apart, holding her mighty warrior posture. Staring down her prey.

He looked at her mother, refusing to help her off the floor, and said, "You better tell your daughter to get the hell out of here!"

But the little warrior would not move. She couldn't hear her mother pleading for her to go back to her room. She only heard the thunder of clouds, the feet of armies by her side, and the thrust of 10,000 angels all around her.

The demon turned back to face his adversary. He looked in astonishment that she hadn't moved.

Not once did the little warrior take her eyes off her prey.

Time was indeed… frozen.

He watched as she motioned with the tip of the knife, gently gliding it from one side of her neck to the other as she proclaimed the words, "I am going to cut you from here to here if you stay in this house one more night! Get out! And don't you ever come back again!"

She meant it.

And he knew it.

The next few seconds seemed like eternity. He did not move.

Time was frozen.

Finally, he broke rank and sheepishly shrugged his shoulders, as if he were not afraid… but his eyes told the truth.

She was no longer a little girl. She was now a warrior. And as this little warrior stared into his eyes, she saw him for who he truly was…powerless. Defeated. Dethroned!

Without looking at her mother, the little warrior slowly turned away and walked back to her room, still holding her promise in her left hand with the boldness that only came from the presence of nations by her side.

From that night forward, I never saw his face again. That would be the last time I saw that demon.

That is… in my childhood.

necessary.

Reflection:

I remember this story like it was yesterday. It was the day I recognized something in me was greater than who was visible on the outside. It was the day I started walking in kingship, as a powerful young girl with a fearless mentality because I knew God stood by my side. From that moment, I knew that no person, nor any spirit, could ever overtake me. It was the day I knew that I would be a leader, a protector, a mighty force for God, and a helper for my family and others.

I was just a child, but I felt the power of nations inside of me. I felt the presence of a mighty warrior.

I became the warrior!

Recommended Reading:

Passages that reference "do not be afraid" or "fear not" are written in the Bible hundreds of times. Take a moment to read some of these passages below:

- *So do not fear, for I am with you; do not be dismayed, for I am your God* (Isaiah 41:10 NIV).
- *Be strong and courageous. Do not be afraid* (Joshua 1:9 NIV).
- *For I the Lord thy God will hold thy right hand, saying unto thee, Fear not; I will help thee* (Isaiah 41:13 KJV).
- *Yea, though I walk through the valley of the shadow of death, I will fear no evil: for thou art with me* (Psalm 23:4 KJV).

- *For God hath not given us the spirit of fear; but of power, and of love, and of a sound mind* (2 Timothy 1:7 KJV).
- *The Lord is my light and my salvation; whom shall I fear? The Lord is the strength of my life; of whom shall I be afraid?* (Psalm 27:1 KJV).
- *Though an army besiege me, my heart will not fear; though war break out against me, even then I will be confident* (Psalm 27:3 NIV).
- *I sought the Lord, and he heard me, and delivered me from all my fears* (Psalm 34:4 KJV).

Assignment:

1. What does each passage mean to you, and how will this impact your life moving forward?

Side Note: For your convenience, a list of nationally recognized organizations that offer confidential support are listed on my website www.ZenjaGlass.com under the Resources/Help tab as a reference only.

[Audio/Video version of this book is available at ZenjaGlass.com]

Chapter 3

Affirmation – Through the Fire

I don't even recognize who I see in the mirror

Because you no longer look like what you've been through.

Who is this person with such a brilliant glow?

The smell from the fire is absent,

And you are no longer bound by what held you down.

How is it possible that you survived the fire?

How is it possible that you overcame all odds against you?

Who taught you how to recycle all your pain

From the blazing furnace

And come forth as pure gold?

Ah, now I understand.

Now I understand why you have such a brilliant glow.

God has refined you,

And you are now His reflection!

[Audio/Video version of this book is available at ZenjaGlass.com]

Chapter 3

Through the Fire

Many years ago, I conducted a brief study on how gold is purified, and the processes were fascinating. One process involves turning up the temperature very high (nearly 2000 degrees Fahrenheit) so that the impurities from the metal would float to the top, leaving pure gold. Another process involves adding very strong acids to gold to dissolve all the impurities so that only pure gold would remain. There is also a process of using electricity. This involves the use of electric currents so that all impurities are removed, leaving pure gold. By the time I completed my research, I concluded one important thing: In order for gold to be purified, it must be refined; it must go through a process to be changed, by releasing what does not belong.

I will never forget when, at a church service, one of our ministers delivered a powerful sermon to encourage the congregation to never let anyone or any situation pull us away from seeking God. He said the top three things that can break a person down, ruin a family, or destroy someone's faith are marriage or relationship issues, financial issues, or health issues. He went on to say that while there are certainly many other areas that can challenge us in life, these three areas tend to be the most common challenges.

I remember that day and that sermon like it was yesterday. I couldn't breathe. I couldn't move. I thought to myself as I looked around the congregation, "My God! I am experiencing all three of these issues. Am I the only person in this building who is experiencing such sorrow, such stress, such disaster... all at the same time?"

necessary.

I thought about my marriage as I sat in church that day. My marriage was in the blazing furnace during that time and we were having arguments on a consistent basis. To say things were bad would be a tremendous understatement. I can't even count the number of times I threatened to leave. This was not how things were supposed to turn out.

We both loved God with all our hearts and we led Bible discussions helping many people make a commitment to follow God. We also helped to restore many marriages on the brink of divorce. In essence, our household was the lighthouse for broken spirits who were on the verge of giving up. It was common practice to host numerous events and Bible studies in our home, helping anyone and feeding anyone who showed up. Then one day we found ourselves going through some of the very trials we were counseling other people through, and falling prey to the very things we warned them about.

How is it possible to love and serve God, yet experience such strange, unexpected fires? It just made no sense to me at all.

And just as I felt I couldn't take on anything else, the fires turned up even hotter in my life. I started experiencing some major financial problems that seemed to grow worse as the economy took a bad turn. We owned a small staffing agency together, and the mounting pressures from depending on one source of income in a fluctuating economy and a failing marriage, were almost too much to bear. I was feeling completely stressed at that time, working late in the evenings and doing everything I knew to avoid a complete financial collapse. No matter how much water I threw on the fire, the flames just seemed to grow higher and higher.

Our first child was born with a chronic medical condition, which made the hospital our second home due to multiple trips on almost a monthly basis throughout his life to manage his intense sickle cell pain. I can't count the number of times I felt so helpless watching my child scream in agony, knowing there was little I could do to take his pain away.

Sometimes his pain was so severe, the doctors would maximize the amount of pain medications they could give him, just to take the edge off his pain. I remember one day I took him swimming, and I had to immediately rush him to the hospital as soon as he got out of the water because the water was too cold for him, and it triggered another sickle cell crisis. He was in such excruciating pain that I ran every red light just to get him to the hospital in time for treatments. I would have traded places with my son in a minute because, as a parent, I would rather endure the pain myself than to see my child suffer.

As I sat in church service that day, I remember thinking to myself, "I don't know anyone who can relate to what I am going through. I keep praying, but nothing is changing. No one understands how hard I am trying to keep things together and how much I am denying myself to take care of everyone else." I felt so drained. So misunderstood. So unloved. So uncared for. So tired. So... exhausted.

So I began to do what most people unknowingly do when life spins out of control: I began to embrace counterfeit gods. Of course, I didn't know that's what I was doing at the time. I still went to church and read my Bible, and prayed whenever I could muster up the strength to pray or cry out to God; but I needed an escape from what I could not control. I needed a happy place, even if it wasn't good for me... even if it was only temporary... even if it actually made things worse.

I used to fantasize quite a bit in my younger years by creating an imaginary world. Because I had a vivid imagination, it was very easy for me to escape from my reality and traumatic events by imagining characters and scenes where I could determine how

necessary.

the story ended. It came as no surprise, as I began to experience some of the most difficult moments in my life as an adult, that I found myself spending pockets of time revisiting those foreign lands. By this time, I had mastered fantasizing because it became a natural part of my life when I was bored, felt unloved or unprotected, or saddened by a situation. It was my own little secret space that brought me comfort and joy when I couldn't find it externally; and I saw nothing wrong with it. After all, I wasn't hurting anyone. Right?

Whether I was going to sleep or sitting alone, I learned how to disconnect from my reality and get lost in another world of romance and make-believe fantasies, where there were no issues—a world that made me feel loved, beautiful, happy, and secure. This fantasy world of false realities became one of my primary escapes. I was never someone who watched a lot of television or movies, so this became my source of entertainment, and to a larger degree, my escape from what I felt was missing in my life.

It took me many years to realize I was playing in Satan's backyard, because those "harmless" fantasies became my escape to the point where it nearly replaced my prayer life and my desire to seek God when I was going through difficult times. I believe imagination and creativity is a gift from God, but nothing should ever take His place on the throne. I got to the point where I would rather lie down or go for a drive and immerse myself in a fantasy, than put in the necessary work to deal with my troubling reality.

In that season of my life, I was consumed with worrying about finances, doing my best to raise four small children, running back and forth to the hospital on a consistent basis, dealing with a marriage that was hanging on by a thread, and trying to take care of everyone else who came to me with an issue or a need. I was just done!

So, what did I do? I found another counterfeit god. I started going to casinos to sit on penny slot machines to completely forget about all my problems. It didn't matter that I didn't have a lot of money. I would sit for hours with a little bit of money just to hear the sound of the machines and escape from the pressures of life. Though my schedule was always very busy with work, motherhood, and what seemed like a million other things, I would take every opportunity I could find to run back to the casino where my troubles were not allowed to enter.

The casino welcomed me with open arms! She lit up a pathway for me to enter with a promise to make me rich overnight and solve all my problems. She gave me friends who sat to my right and to my left on penny slot machines while we gambled away our coins, laughing and pretending all was well. We all had hopes of winning a jackpot and riding off into the sunset to finally live life to the fullest! It didn't matter that on any given day, we were total strangers, rooting for each other. In those moments, we were best friends as we cheered each other on whenever one of us entered a jackpot or a bonus round.

Going to the casino quickly became, by far, my most fun leisure activity. It was so much fun, so freeing, so away from my reality, that it was favored over just about any other event. And any time I was able to save up a few extra dollars, I always kept it aside for my next casino adventure because the penny slot machines always greeted me and welcomed me to "Come on down!" and try my luck.

You might be tempted to think: "So what's the problem? There is nothing wrong with a little bit of fun now and then."

Well, on one end, I totally agree with that, but herein lies the problem: Anytime I was bored, angry, feeling unloved, under financial pressure, etc., I found myself wanting to go to the casino INSTEAD of running into the arms of God. Then, I found myself

necessary.

lying about how much I'd spent, and always longing for the next trip the moment a problem arose in my life. I would get highly defensive if anyone challenged me about why I wanted to go. I was a pro at justifying why I deserved to go. I reasoned that I didn't go often, didn't spend much money, and didn't do anything else for fun in my life.

But when I returned home, my reality was always there to greet me at the door.

The problem for me was why I went to the casino. I went to run away from my reality. I went to solve my financial woes. I went to flee from the pressure I was under. I went to find peace and happiness. I went to forget all the pains from my past. I ran to casinos as an escape because I was afraid of what the future held for me. Instead of laying my pain on the altar of God and seeking His divine guidance and help, I chose to numb it... if only for a moment.

When we are not filled with the knowledge and power of God, something else has to fill that void. Yet those counterfeit gods NEVER hold true to their promises. They always leave us feeling lonely, hopeless, and filled with anxiety and stress. Counterfeit gods always point us to alternative solutions such as gambling, drugs, pouring ourselves into our jobs, worshipping relationships out of desperation or fear of rejection, the love of money, and so on.

God allowed me to reach a very low place in my life. I felt so powerless. I was ashamed of who I had become. But you couldn't tell that from the outside. On the outside, I looked like I had it all together— nice house, married, my own business, a master's degree... the works! But on the inside, I was filled with despair, loneliness, fear, worry, anxiety, stress, and feelings of being unloved.

Through the Fire

To make matters worse, in my pride and arrogance, I walked around as if everything were fine. I still had an image to keep up, and with the exception of opening up to a few people at my church, I didn't want anyone to think I wasn't strong enough or smart enough to survive and figure things out on my own. After all, that was the story of my life. Only this time, that didn't work for me. I was out of answers. I was tired. The fire was too hot at that point.

I had already tried just about everything I knew to do to turn my circumstances around. You name it, and I probably tried it. Individual counseling, marriage counseling, working long hours to make more money, trying to force changes to happen, going to church, praying, cursing people out. You name it, I did it. I tried everything I knew to do. And nothing seemed to work. The fire only grew hotter and hotter.

I couldn't even find many friends who I felt could relate to all the simultaneous pressures and pains I was experiencing at that time. Their version of a tough day seemed equivalent to complaining about a melted ice cream sundae to me. Most of the time, I didn't even bother to venture into deep topics with others, because I felt if one more happy person told me to just "trust in God," I was going to hit them!

I got tired of hearing the same repeated messages from those whom I felt were not in the fires, nor have ever experienced such blazing fires in their lives. I know it was not right for me to think that way. Life has now shown me that our individual experiences are all relative, and just because someone can't relate to our pain, doesn't mean they haven't experienced pain themselves. But none of that mattered at that time. I just did not have any patience for what I categorized as bubble-gum conversations.

I tried talking to God, but He wasn't speaking back to me. He wasn't solving anything. He wasn't moving fast enough. At least that's what I felt at the time. I would pray to Him, cry out to Him,

necessary.

and feel good for a moment, but nothing significant happened after that. In fact, at times things seemed to get worse! So, I held on to my counterfeit gods because at least they made me feel happy. At least they pretended to care.

But, as with all alternative, counterfeit gods, running to them only made matters worse. The more I escaped to temporary pleasures, the greater my problems intensified. Soon I began "chasing" the money that I had lost in the casinos. To no surprise, that created even more issues in my household. And the one thing I thought was completely harmless, began to take the place of my prayer life because it became easier for me to fantasize about the life I wanted, than to accept my reality and begin to do the real work that was needed for my refinement.

I could no longer keep up with the image I worked so hard to protect, because the fires began to spread into my workplace and into just about every area of my life. I even lost some friends, and in my anger I said hurtful words to people I love. Words that can never be taken back. Words that broke relationships and burned down bridges that took years to rebuild.

I wish I could say the fires subsided at that point, but that did not happen. Just when I thought the blazing furnace couldn't possibly get any hotter; as purifying gold enters its final stage of the melting process, my mother's health started rapidly declining and she began experiencing congestive heart failure and a series of other health conditions that left her bedridden and barely able to communicate.

My mother had to be relocated to a facility several hours away from us because that was the closest location equipped to handle her chronic health conditions. Because I am the eldest child and served as my mother's representative, I consistently received phone calls from her care facility about everything, ranging from her physical needs to her declining health emergencies.

Through the Fire

I remember thinking, "This is just completely ridiculous at this point! Who deals with all these issues at the same time?" My mother was an amazing woman of God; and once her health began to rapidly decline, I don't know if there ever was a time in my life when I felt so lonely and exhausted. If I wasn't at the hospital taking care of my son, I was either working, taking care of someone else, or taking a call from my mother's hospital. I truly believe there are times in life when the pressure is so great, and the furnace is so hot, that it almost becomes laughable. For me, that was one of those seasons.

I was in such disbelief of all the fires I was experiencing in that long season of my life, that finally I had to throw my hands up and fully surrender it all to God. My life was out of control and I needed help. I needed more than experiencing His presence once a week during a Sunday church service. I had to surrender to the refinement process He was allowing me to pass through by releasing what no longer belonged, so that I could come forth as pure gold. I had to be transformed and allow God to pour new wine into new wineskins (Matthew 9:16). I had to have more of Him... and less of me (John 3:30).

So, I went all in. I decided to put pressure on God's integrity to see if He truly would do what He said He would do if I fully surrendered to Him. I started attending a weekly Bible study session that focused heavily on teaching me how to sit and listen to the Holy Spirit. I will discuss more about those Bible sessions in the next chapter, because I certainly did not welcome them with open arms. But I think it is important here to note a few key points that I learned.

I remember reading a passage: "All things are permitted, but not all things are of benefit. All things are permitted, but not all things build people up" (1 Corinthians 10:23 NASB).

One of the most valuable lessons I learned was how we process pain. If we don't run to God, we stay in a painful cycle after being

necessary.

triggered by an event, reacting the same way, and ending up with the same results.

I learned more about Satan, the deceiver, the accuser, and the enemy of God. I also learned how he manipulates situations and roams around looking for people to devour (1 Peter 5:8).

I learned that there was tremendous power that lived inside of me: that is, Jesus Christ [Yeshua], the source of all knowledge and wisdom (Colossians 2:2-3). This was not my first time hearing any of this. I had been a Christian for many years prior. I'd simply... forgotten!

I forgot who I was in the sight of God (Galatians 3:26).

I forgot I had power to stand in the midst of great trials and storms (1 Corinthians 10:13).

I forgot the Holy Spirit speaks and gives wisdom and guidance (John 14:26).

And I certainly forgot how deceptive Satan is (Revelation 12:9).

I began to spend a few minutes sitting in my closet every night to simply pour out my heart to God. Within a few weeks, those minutes turned into hours, and much of that time was simply sitting silently in His presence. Most of the time, I was too weak and too exhausted to pray, so I just sat in His presence... and listened. To be completely transparent, the vast majority of the time, I heard nothing at all. So, I just sat.

Then, little by little, God began to reveal hidden secrets to me. I soon replaced fruitless arguments with Bible study. I started praying instead of fantasizing, meditating on biblical passages instead of running to counterfeit gods, playing gospel music and spiritual songs throughout my day instead of allowing my mind to play negative narratives, controlling my tongue by remembering scriptures about God's faithfulness and His protection instead of always feeling the need to defend my character, and fighting in the Spirit to get my strength, joy, and peace from God instead of making the casino my primary option for happiness.

Strange things began to happen in my life as I repented and let go of my counterfeit gods, and instead, aligned my life with the word of God. I began to experience a level of peace that I couldn't explain. It didn't make sense for me to feel peace when my circumstances hadn't changed that much. It was a peace that surpassed all understanding (Philippians 4:6-7) because instead of focusing on what was wrong in my life, God kept me occupied with gladness of heart (Ecclesiastes 5:20). Not only did God begin to fill me with inner peace, He began to change the way I viewed my life. And even better than that, God had the audacity to begin to change my life!

Little did I know, the hand of God was always masterfully at work, standing with me in the fires, refining me, chipping away at my pride and arrogance, building my testimony, molding my character, teaching me perseverance, planting empathy and compassion in my heart for others, and purifying me to come forth as pure gold so that I could give hope to the brokenhearted and encourage others who stand in blazing fires.

In this secret place, God showed me how to walk in His power when I had no strength of my own. He taught me how to stand and watch His deliverance. He miraculously gave me strategies to use less than $200 to launch another business, eventually hire several full-time employees, and offer support to wonderful causes that help children with chronic medical conditions, and kids who are victims of human trafficking. And many years later, in 2020, God placed it on my heart to launch *Unlocking Greatness Podcast with Zenja Glass*, a motivational podcast that has spread all over the world and helped hundreds of thousands of people to never give up in life by inspiring them to pursue their dreams and draw closer to God.

necessary.

I had absolutely no intention of pouring out my heart on social media, because I worked with corporate executives and I didn't know how it would impact my business, or my life, if people found me being open and vulnerable about my battles on the internet as I shared my stories to help others. I quickly dismissed that fear because I will never be ashamed to speak about the goodness of the Lord! I knew the sound of His voice, and no amount of riches or praises from others could ever take the place of serving and honoring God in my life.

I have learned that even when we go through the fires, we are able to fight in the Spirit and extinguish the flaming arrows from the enemy (Ephesians 6:10-20). God is able to turn our lives around and use our testimonies to help others, as we bring glory and honor to Him.

In closing, I want to stress an important point: no matter what fires you are going through, I plead with you to please seek help (spiritually and professionally) if you find yourself struggling in life. Please know that God loves you, and don't ever believe that you have gone so far away from Him that He will not welcome you with open arms. God specializes in using our messes for His good. Let Him use you!

We all have sinned and fall short (Romans 3:23), and I know firsthand how guilty and embarrassing it can be when we feel we have let ourselves or our families down. But know that God is a loving God and He cares for you! Nothing you have been through will be wasted. We are all here for each other and our good and bad experiences can be used for the glory of God to lift others from dark places. But we must be willing to get the help needed and allow God to use us. If no one has told you this, I want you to know... you are loved!

It doesn't matter what anyone may have said to you, you are valuable in the sight of God! If you are reading or listening to these words, you must know, it is not too late to get help and allow God to change your life in ways you can only imagine. The devil is a liar! It is not too late! Don't believe the lies the enemy might be trying to feed you. No matter how bad things might seem right now, you must believe that God still loves YOU!

I was fortunate to have a praying mother who reminded me, just before she died, of these words that I will now pass on to you. She said, "Baby, if you can learn to praise God in the middle of your storms, you will praise your way out of the storms. That's the secret! The secret is praise!"

We may not always know why we go through the fires, but we do know who stands with us in the fires!

Reflection:

It's hard to believe these few pages in this chapter reflect nearly two decades of my life. I am almost without words as I reflect on how much God has pulled me through. God is a Waymaker and a Miracle Worker!

Ironically, all these years later, one of my offices now sits on top of a plaza and a small casino is below me. By the grace of God, what was once my counterfeit god has now become my footstool!

To God be all the glory!

Recommended Reading:

- *But he knows the way that I take; when he has tested me, I will come forth as gold* (Job 23:10 NIV).

necessary.

- *And God is faithful; he will not let you be tempted beyond what you can bear. But when you are tempted, he will also provide a way out so that you can endure it* (1 Corinthians 10:13 NIV).
- *When you pass through the waters, I will be with you; and when you pass through the rivers, they will not sweep over you. When you walk through the fire, you will not be burned; the flames will not set you ablaze. For I am the Lord, your God, the Holy One of Israel, your Savior* (Isaiah 43:2-3 NIV).
- *For he will command his angels concerning you to guard you in all your ways* (Psalm 91:11 NIV).
- *But the Comforter which is the Holy Ghost, whom the Father will send in my name, he shall teach you all things, and bring all things to your remembrance, whatsoever I have said unto you* (John 14:26 KJV).
- *Do not be anxious about anything, but in every situation, by prayer and petition, with thanksgiving, present your requests to God. And the peace of God, which transcends all understanding, will guard your hearts and your minds in Christ Jesus* (Philippians 4:6 NIV).
- *They seldom reflect on the days of their life, because God keeps them occupied with gladness of heart* (Ecclesiastes 5:20 NIV).
- *No weapon that is formed against thee shall prosper* (Isaiah 54:17 KJV).
- *You shall have no other gods before me* (Exodus 20:3 NIV).
- *If any of you lacks wisdom, you should ask God, who gives generously to all without finding fault, and it will be given to you* (James 1:5 NIV).

Assignment:

Please read the entire story of "The Parable of the Lost Son" (some Bible translations refer to this as, "The Prodigal Son") and pay careful attention to how the father (representing the love of God) ran to his son (representing us) and welcomed him back after he made bad choices in life. This story can be found in Luke 15:11-32.

1. What have you learned about God's faithfulness when you go through the fire?

2. Can you identify any counterfeit gods in your life? If so, what are they? Are you willing to seek help? If so, please make the first step today and seek help.

3. Do you have a secret place where you can get away from others and sit in the presence of God to meditate on His words and pray? If not, write down some possible locations where you would be most comfortable to sit or walk alone. Then, begin that journey of simply sitting with God. Even if it is only for a few minutes each day, sit with Him, and listen to what He has to say.

[Audio/Video version of this book is available at ZenjaGlass.com]

Chapter 4

Affirmation – Seek God First?

Even when I don't feel your presence

And the troubles of life seem to overwhelm me

I will search for you.

I will search for you as though for hidden treasures

Because your presence in my life is of far more value than

Anything I can ever hold in my hands.

Even when I don't understand your plan for my life

And everything in me wants to give up

I will search for you.

You are worth searching for.

You are my Deliverer.

My Waymaker.

My Refuge.

My only God!

[Audio/Video version of this book is available at ZenjaGlass.com]

Chapter 4

Seek God First?

I will never forget the day I went to a women's Bible study group led by some amazing facilitators. It was based on the book, *Spiritual Discovery - 7 Principles for Spiritual Growth,* by co-authors Virginia Lefler and Kathy Heinen. I was there to talk about my problems, my issues with my marriage, my concerns with my children, my financial woes, issues with people who hurt me, and so much more. I just knew that if my circumstances changed, then my life would be better and I could finally experience the peace and joy I was so desperately seeking.

So there I was sitting in a Bible study group and ready to talk about everything that everyone had done wrong to me. They gave an overview of the topics we would be discussing, such as revisiting our childhood memories and taking God with us to painful times in our lives so that we can go back and get the truth. Then, they started talking about the importance of sitting in silence before God and listening to the Holy Spirit.

After everyone in the group had their turn to share about their circumstances, the facilitator of the group had the nerve to focus the discussion on the importance of seeking God first. It took everything in me to keep from completely going off on her! I thought to myself, "How is it possible to seek God first when my finances are falling apart? How is it possible to resort to meditation and prayer when my marriage was on the brink of divorce? How in the world is it possible to walk in faith when I am dealing with major health issues in my family? And who has time

necessary.

to seek God first when their children are going through things and life seems to be falling completely apart?"

It was just too much to comprehend because I felt I couldn't add anything else to my *To-Do* list. And yes, in case you are wondering, I went to church on a consistent basis, I loved God, and I prayed and read my Bible and did all that stuff we as Christians are supposed to do. But taking on that stance of sitting with God and seeking His divine direction in the midst of my storms was just too passive for me. My situations required taking fast actions because nothing seemed to be getting better in my life. I was consumed with worrying about my circumstances, and I didn't see how seeking God first was going to solve anything!

By the end of that first session, I was so angry!

Who in the world has time to be still when they are doing their best to keep their heads above water?

Those were my thoughts, and I saw absolutely nothing wrong with them.

I remember thinking to myself, *They must not have any real issues they are dealing with if that's the best solution they could come up with!*

Who has time to sit still and fight in the Spirit when chaos is all around them? Is that even possible?

And in regard to revisiting my past, that was a big NO for me! Who on earth has time to focus on their past when they can barely breathe in their present atmosphere?

I thought again to myself, *Did they not hear a single word out of my mouth? I attended these Bible sessions to come from under my pain, not to SIT in it!*

So I left. Disturbed. Irritated. Saddened. And very angry!

Seek God First?

I left that Bible study session and I distinctly recall telling the facilitator, "I won't be back. These women are too weak for me to deal with. I have major issues going on and I don't see what my past has to do with any of this, nor do I have the luxury of sitting silently before God and doing nothing when all hell has broken loose in my life! I pray to God all the time. He is the only reason I have made it this far, but I don't have time just to be sitting around in silence, digging up the past, and waiting for some magical answer to appear!"

I went on to say, "First, I need to take care of all the issues in my life so I can have the strength, the peace, and the willpower to even think about focusing on myself, my past, and, of all things, sitting in silence before God. Once I have figured out what I need to do, then I will have enough peace in my life to do all that other stuff!"

My marriage was falling completely apart, and by that time I felt that it was nearly impossible to avoid all the arguments we were having on a consistent basis. I just could not understand how it was possible to be married, yet feel so alone. We went from being a lighthouse, guiding and mending other families, to becoming like strangers living under the same roof, and for a period of time, in separate rooms! We were giving our love and attention to others, while neglecting our marriage. And to be clear, I certainly did my part to contribute to the divisiveness, lack of love, and discord that nearly destroyed us. Our families were greatly divided, I had to end some friendships, and to make matters worse, our children were being negatively impacted, and it influenced their behavior at home and at school. It was all a huge mess! I became very angry and resentful because no matter how hard I tried to make things better, nothing seemed to change.

As you can probably now imagine, the very thought of going back to those Bible sessions and sitting with women I perceived to be

necessary.

weak was not something I had in mind because I was convinced that if I went that route, I would become a doormat for others to walk over and treat as they please.

I was not about to let that happen!

So I left, and I was adamant about not going back again. The only advice I felt I needed at that time was how to fix or end my marriage, how to get my hands on some money, and how to help my children. The thought of sitting still and putting things in the hands of God, and the thought of working on *me* when I was trying to correct everyone else, really ticked me off!

But over the next few days, God allowed the heat in my marriage, and in other areas of my life, to turn up very high. I was feeling so out of control that I thought to myself, *I have two options: I either need to take my butt back to that Bible study group and learn how to fully surrender everything over to God and walk in His power, or I am going to end up in jail!*

Reluctantly, I went back to that Bible session the following week. I was a little embarrassed because I told them I wouldn't return again, but I am so grateful I showed up and began to do the work that would forever change my life. I laid my weapons down at the foot of the cross and finally surrendered it all to God. I am a living witness; my life has never been the same since that day!

All along, I had it backward. I thought fighting in the flesh was my only option. I had no idea, fighting in the Spirit was the primary solution to most of my issues.

I thought all my circumstances needed to change first, in order for me to walk in power, peace, and joy. I was wrong. I never really knew the greatest, necessary change was always within me. Just to be clear, I absolutely had to set up some healthy boundaries, but the greatest impact in every area of my life started when I made the intentional decision to seek God first.

Seek God First?

I was already familiar with the Bible passage: "But seek ye first the kingdom of God, and his righteousness; and all these things shall be added unto you" (Matthew 6:33 KJV). It was nice to read. It sounded great, but I don't know if I ever really believed in the integrity of that passage because somewhere in the back of my mind I thought, *It sounds good, but does that really happen?*

Never in a million years did I ever believe taking time to go back in my past would be such a healing journey. Revisiting my childhood was the one thing I initially took a strong stand against when I went back to that group. I didn't see a need to deal with pain from childhood trauma, and I certainly did not see how it could produce anything of value to me as an adult. Besides, I already had enough on my plate, so why on earth would I want to walk down memory lane and add more pressure to my life?

But this was different. The facilitator reminded me that I didn't have to go back alone. I will never forget when she whispered to me, "This time, you get to take God with you." While this process was not easy, it certainly was healing because, through meditation and prayer, I was able to go back to painful or fearful moments that shaped me in the past and find my truth. I never knew the truth could free me!

For example, when I took God back with me to challenging seasons of my life, I would say, "God, is it true that I was alone during that time of my life? Is it true that I was the protector of my family at such a young age?" Then, I would simply sit in His presence, listen to His response, and receive the truth.

I must admit, it took some time and a lot of patience before His truths were revealed to me because I struggled with sitting silently after praying... just to listen. I was so used to praying and then getting up and moving on in life. It was odd for me to pray, ask God for His truth, and then sit... and wait for Him to speak to me.

necessary.

When I first tried this, it felt so awkward. I remember telling the facilitator that I didn't hear anything at all. In fact, I even questioned if perhaps I was answering my own questions. But then there was a moment I will never forget. I meditated and prayed to God about a very painful experience in my life. Then I sat in silence for a long time and waited for His response. I will never forget hearing this inward, gentle voice that began to give me truths—truths that I never knew before. It was in those moments that I was able to let go and no longer fear my past. I was finally able to embrace my story.

I also learned why it was so easy for me as an adult to worry about finances. It was a spirit of scarcity that I never left behind. When I was a child, things were always scarce because my mother received public aid until she completed college, and that wasn't until later in my life, around the same time I graduated from college. Though we never went a day hungry, I recall eating at food shelters, getting meals from churches, and receiving food donations from local organizations. I know how powdered eggs, powdered milk, and government cheese taste because my young mother did her best to raise three kids on $192 a month. She was just a child herself when she had me. Her mother passed away when she was only a little girl. My mother did her best to raise her children and provide for her kids with the knowledge she had at that time. And I love her for it!

As a young girl, I remember moving 22 times in one year because my mother was running away from a very abusive relationship and, at times, couldn't pay rent. I am sure there were probably other reasons as well, but I was too young to recall all that was happening. I made a game of it by remembering all the street addresses where we resided. I'll never forget the day I told my aunt I could remember all 22 addresses where we lived, and she broke down in tears. At the time, I didn't understand why she

Seek God First?

responded that way. I thought she would be proud that I could recite our last 22 or so home addresses that year.

As an adult, I now understand the grief she felt in her heart for us. I never paid much attention to that season of my life until I started getting stressed about my finances as an adult during turbulent times. And, believe it or not, I stressed about my finances in good times as well. It was as if I couldn't enjoy the good times because I was always waiting for something unexpected to happen.

I had to go back to many of those scary places and take God with me to find His truth. To seek healing. To get my power back and to bring it to the present.

My past explained why, as an adult, I worked diligently and pushed myself to go above expectations by excelling in everything I did. I always worked long hours and pushed myself to go beyond what most people would do, because deep inside I was fearful of not having enough. Eventually, I resigned from my corporate job and became a fearless entrepreneur and business owner. But no matter how much I achieved or acquired, I lived in constant fear of scarcity and instability. As the economy began to tumble, I started worrying about my finances; and without realizing it, I defaulted to my old childhood memories when we moved from house to house. I started making decisions out of panic, instead of being led by the Holy Spirit and walking in wisdom.

I am so grateful to have learned the importance of seeking the truth from God. For example, I remember asking Him, "God, is it true that I won't have enough to provide for my family now?" I had to get His truth so that I could walk in faith, make wise decisions, and no longer be chained by my past. It was so freeing to finally debunk the lies Satan was feeding me. His objective was

necessary.

always to rob me of my tomorrow by keeping me stuck in fear today.

Don't ever let the enemy rob you of your tomorrow!

I also learned quite a bit about why I responded in certain ways when I felt disrespected. Because I saw my mother get abused several times in my life as a child, I was adamant that I was never going to allow anyone to do anything I perceived as walking over me. Though I did my very best to treat people well, the moment I was triggered by anything or any statement that launched me back to those painful childhood memories of my mom, I was immediately ready for war! I was determined to never become that vulnerable version of my mother.

As a result, I loved hard but I fought even harder! I didn't hesitate to defend myself or my character if anyone hurt my feelings or disrespected me. I also didn't hesitate to defend anyone who was not courageous enough to speak up for themselves. And while some of those actions were honorable, it also inserted me into a lot of battles that didn't have my name on it, because I was always quick to rush to the defense of the underdog.

When the Bible teaches us to "do everything without grumbling or arguing" (Philippians 2:14 NIV), I thought that was unrealistic. How is it even possible to have that kind of self-control if you feel someone is not considering your feelings or does not have your best intention in mind? I thought my only choices were to be completely passive or aggressive, depending on the situation. I had no idea I had a choice to rise above challenging circumstances, and let God shift the atmosphere. I had no idea that kind of power lived inside of me!

I didn't know it was possible to thrive and have inward peace without validation from others. That is part of the reason I got so frustrated. No matter how hard I tried to love people and help others, I couldn't force them to change nor to love me. This created a very toxic environment in some areas of my life, especially in my marriage because I was adamant about fixing what was on the outside so that I could have peace on the inside.

If you can't force people to change, how on earth are you supposed to focus on yourself and thrive in a negative environment? The obvious answer for most people is to just leave, right? And I do not stand in judgment on anyone who has walked away from negative situations.

But for me, walking away from everything and everyone who frustrated or disappointed me was the easy part. Heck, I moved 22 times in one year as a child, so walking away, being alone, or starting life over again is a fairly easy concept for me. But after much prayer, I chose to stay planted, right there in the midst of the fires, and begin the necessary work... on me.

As I drew closer to God, spending countless hours in prayer, Bible study, and Bible meditation, I learned some powerful secrets that changed my life. I learned that as we elevate into higher realms with God by developing a genuine, intimate relationship with Him, we have the power living inside of us not only to be transformed but to change the entire atmosphere everywhere we go!

We have the power to be self-controlled and walk in peace and authority everywhere we go! We have the power to disengage from foolish arguments by speaking our truth and developing healthy boundaries. And because of the favor God has over our lives, we have the power to thrive in challenging seasons.

As a practical example, I never knew I had the power to have a joyful, peaceful day even if someone had a bad attitude or used the silent treatment as a way to discourage me. I always thought I had to join that dance by matching their negativity or by trying to win the favor of someone who clearly didn't want to communicate with me. I never knew I was giving other people

necessary.

the power to determine what kind of day I would have because if they were in a bad mood I naturally followed suit. Have you ever felt this way?

Have you ever felt like you had to brace yourself before walking into your workplace or your home because you didn't know what mood someone might be in? It can be very discouraging, right? Your demeanor may totally change from happy to dismal because you already know someone will have an issue with something or, perhaps, be in a negative mood.

I didn't know I could rise above my circumstance with Jesus Christ [Yeshua] by my side, and look at what was happening, almost in great amazement, as I watched what the enemy was trying to do. He was trying to lure me to the dance floor and grieve my spirit. I soon realized I didn't have to participate in that dance with anyone! I had a choice to exit the dance floor–to walk away with grace, dignity, and power, as I praised and worshiped God, instead of responding to negativity with negativity.

So, instead of reacting as I naturally would, I simply went higher by developing healthy boundaries for myself and inviting the presence of God into the room. Instead of joining the dance, I read my Bible, went on a walk, prayed in my closet, worked on a creative plan God gave me, played my favorite worship songs and sang to God with a huge smile on my face, and so on. I did whatever it took to bring the presence of God into the environment so that I would change. And when I changed, the atmosphere had to adjust to me! The new me, that is. The new me, who rose to a higher level. The new me, who refused to bow down and dance with the enemy!

Looking back, it seems funny to me that I thought running to God was a sign of weakness. I was so sure He would turn me into a doormat, and to be honest, for a moment, I certainly felt that way. My version of walking in love and humility looked like a

Seek God First?

passive, weak person who let anyone do anything to them, but that was not the case at all; nor was it true of the women from my Bible study group who I thought were too weak for me to befriend. Those women turned out to be some of the strongest, wisest, and most amazing women I know to this day!

As I reflect on those earlier years when my pain was so deep and nothing in me wanted to start looking inward to begin the necessary journey from within, I am so grateful I didn't turn away the hand of God. Seeking God first led me to repent of my sins, including pride, anger, idolatry, and discord. I learned how to stand as a woman of God, set healthy boundaries in my life, and show compassion, while walking in love, power, authority, and in humility. I didn't know that combination was even possible!

I gained the power not only to stand in the fires but to thrive in life in ways I never could have imagined. I gained peace in the storms. I gained love in the absence of love. I gained character by learning to persevere. I gained influence to inspire the brokenhearted by refusing to let my pain go to waste. I gained the secret of praising my way out of the storms. I gained far more joy in my soul. And, most importantly, I gained a relationship with God in higher realms of the Spirit than I ever knew was possible!

I don't know your situation, but I can only imagine that some of you may be thinking, "Well, I've been praying all these years and things are still the same." I certainly felt that way at times. And, if I can be completely transparent, there are still some situations I have prayed about for many years that remain unchanged. But I have changed. And I am no longer chained to it!

I serve as a living witness when I tell you, it is possible to grow from dark places. And it is possible to thrive in the valleys, in the very presence of your enemies, even when the challenges of life seem overwhelming. God is masterful at rescuing those who call on Him. He specializes in making a way out of no way! He knows

necessary.

the way out. He knows not only how you can stand, but just as importantly, where you should stand.

I plead with you, as one who has overcome tremendous obstacles and grown in dark places, to seek God first. Seek and "love the Lord thy God with all thy heart, and with all thy soul, and with all thy strength, and with all thy mind" (Luke 10:27 KJV).

When you seek God first in your life, watch how He defends His integrity and honors His promises in your life!

Before I close this chapter, I have to stress the importance of taking care of yourself and seeking professional help if you are being abused in any area of your life. Your safety, including your physical and mental health, is very important.

Reflection:

I could not comprehend how a battle could be won on my knees. That looked so weak to me when I was in the middle of the battlefield. I didn't understand how a war could be fought with weapons I could not hold in my hand. But I was so desperate for my life to change—so desperate for a better version of me—that I had to seek God first and see what He could do in my life.

I never thought I would ever get to the point where I could say, "Dear Lord, you don't have to change anything. Just take me higher with you, where your power, joy, peace, and treasures are in abundance, and let me be used for your good will."

Perhaps this is why I love the Apostle Paul, who was inflicted with a thorn in his flesh. He begged the Lord to take it away, but Jesus said, "My grace is sufficient for you, for my power is made perfect in weakness" (2 Corinthians 12:9 NIV). Paul went on to say, "For when I am weak, then I am strong" (2 Corinthians 12:10 NIV).

Seek God First?

Recommended Reading:

- *"...You will seek me and find me when you seek me with all your heart. I will be found by you," declares the Lord* (Jeremiah 29:13-14 NIV).
- *"...Test me in this," says the Lord Almighty, "and see if I will not throw open the floodgates of heaven and pour out so much blessing that there will not be room enough to store it..."* (Malachi 3:10 NIV).
- *Trust in the Lord with all thine heart; and lean not unto thine own understanding. In all thy ways acknowledge him, and he shall direct thy paths* (Proverbs 3:5-6 KJV).
- *God is faithful; he will not let you be tempted beyond what you can bear... he will also provide a way out so that you can endure it* (1 Corinthians 10:13 NIV).
- Please read one of my favorite passages my mother taught me before she passed away. It is titled, "Do Not Worry" (Matthew 6:25-34). I encourage you to read the entire passage.

Assignment:

1. What challenges are you facing right now?

2. What can you implement from this chapter to help you as you move forward?

3. Can you identify any areas in your life you want to improve so that you can develop a deeper, more intimate relationship with God? If so, be specific.

necessary.

4. Write a brief summary about all the passages from the recommended reading. When you have completed this, take some time to read your summary aloud as often as needed so that you can be reminded why it is important to seek God first in every area of your life.

Chapter 5

Affirmation – The Pruning Season

This is my season!

It has finally arrived!

And no one can take it away!

Finally, I am reaping the rewards God stored up for me!

Finally, the mountains are moving!

You may not understand why tears of joy are flowing from my eyes.

You didn't witness my midnight cries and prayers for better days.

But O' how the seasons have now changed!

God has shown me my labor was not in vain.

This is my season!

I shall rejoice and be glad in it!

Thank you, God!

My season has finally arrived!

[Audio/Video version of this book is available at ZenjaGlass.com]

Chapter 5

The Pruning Season

What happens when God, the Gardener, starts the pruning season in our lives to prepare us for our season of harvest? Can you recognize the harvest is coming when the Gardener begins to cut away what is no longer needed in your life? Can you hold on and trust your harvest is ahead when everything around you seems to fall away? It has taken me well over 50 years to finally understand a very simple, yet challenging concept about the season... before the harvest season: Because He loves me, He also prunes me!

Some of the most challenging moments in my life have produced my greatest growth, but I would be lying to you if I told you that I enjoyed all those seasons of pruning. In fact, it was during some of those painful seasons that I wondered if God really knew, or even cared about, what was happening to me.

Pruning hurts. It cuts. It removes that which does not belong. Pruning ended some relationships in my life. Pruning uprooted and relocated me. At times, pruning left me feeling isolated, unloved, and confused because I just couldn't understand why so much discomfort was happening in my life. I was so focused on what was being cut away that I couldn't see who I was becoming.

It's easy for me to justify trouble coming into my life if I know I am dealing with consequences from my own actions, such as

necessary.

doing something I had no business doing in the first place. Then I could say to myself, "Ok. I brought this upon myself." But when I was doing my best to serve others, teach others about the love of Jesus Christ, and honor God in my life, and trouble still came my way, that just made no sense to me whatsoever! So, it must have been the enemy that was messing with me, right? After all, the thief comes to steal, kill, and destroy (John 10:10) and he roams around looking for someone to devour (1 Peter 5:8). Surely, he must have sneaked in when God wasn't looking... or did he?

John 15:1-2 NIV states: "I am the true vine and my Father is the gardener. He cuts off every branch in me that bears no fruit, while every branch that does bear fruit he prunes so that it will be even more fruitful."

Many Bible scholars believe this passage is in reference to bearing the fruit of the Spirit (Galatians 5:22-23), and some claim it is referring to making disciples as Jesus Christ calls us to do (Matthew 28:19). My purpose in citing this scripture is not to debate the intention of the passage, but to discuss the analogy Jesus used and how we can apply it to our lives.

Why in the world would God prune every branch that *does* bear fruit? The Bible teaches us, "In all things God works for the good of those who love him" (Romans 8:28 NIV). But why prune what is already bearing fruit?

Those were some of the questions I pondered in my heart when I expected to walk into my harvest season. Yet the Gardener showed up unexpectedly and began to prune areas of my life, bringing storms, ripping branches away that were no longer a part of my destiny, uprooting the weeds to expose truths, and changing my entire environment to a point where nothing seemed familiar any longer. It was as if the Gardener came in, without warning, dug me up, cut away most of what I thought was beautiful, and completely changed the landscape by planting me in better soil.

No matter how much I prayed, rebuked the devil, read my Bible, and cried myself to sleep too many times to count, God did not stop cutting away at what was no longer needed for the next season of my life. He broke off branches I thought I needed for my survival. He cut away leaves that I thought gave me protection. He uprooted me from the dry soil I was so comfortable in, and planted me by the streams.

It was painful. And at times, frightening. I didn't understand why He put me through so much… just to grow me. And I certainly didn't understand that He was preparing me for a greater harvest. Can anyone relate to this?

Can you relate to being uprooted and planted in unfamiliar territory, and all that you thought you could rely on was no longer a part of your life? Seems a bit harsh, doesn't it? It made me wonder, *Is the pruning process really necessary?*

As I pondered this question, I decided to conduct some research about the pruning process, specifically about grape vines, to get an understanding of how I could apply this passage to my life. The shortest conclusion from my research is this: Pruning has to be done at the right time to avoid damaging or delaying the maturity of the fruit. If a gardener wants to maximize the crop, the branches have to be pruned to ensure it will continue to grow and produce ripe grapes each year. If the pruning process ever stops, or is delayed for an extended period of time, fewer grapes are produced as a result.

necessary.

The more I researched the pruning process, the more I understood the wisdom of a good gardener and the importance of pruning the branches to produce more growth and, if I could dare say so, to protect the fruit. While this may not satisfy most naysayers, nor be the answer to every pain we have ever experienced, it can certainly help us to grasp the concept of being pruned to grow for the harvest ahead.

The question we all must answer is: Can we trust the Good Gardener? Can we trust that He knows what He is doing? Can we trust that He has prepared a harvest for us, and He prunes us to produce His good will in our lives?

Looking back, I realize I gave Satan way too much credit because if any pain or discomfort occurred in my life I always thought it was the enemy at work. I wasn't mature enough to consider if, perhaps, there were times the Good Gardener was simply at work, preparing me for the seasons ahead. I guess that's why the Bible teaches us to always rejoice in the Lord (Philippians 4:4), because we know that even in our suffering, God has plans to prosper us and not to harm us (Jeremiah 29:11).

If you are in a pruning season right now, and the Good Gardener is cutting away in your life, please know you are not alone. God has not forgotten about you. Our Father is a very skilled Gardener. He knows what He is doing, and even when you don't feel His presence, He sees you. He is with you. He is masterfully working it all out.

My life is a living witness. The Good Gardener showed up unexpectedly and tore everything down! Every altar. Every person I depended on. Everything I thought I could rely on from my own strength. He tore it all down. It was only in my most challenging seasons of great uncertainties and sorrows that I began to grow from dark places, as He placed me in fertile soil and removed what was no longer needed in my life.

I've come to realize there are some pruning processes we may never understand until we meet Him on that great day in heaven. But I want to encourage you to hold on to His unchanging hands and trust the Good Gardener has not taken His eyes off of you. Trust that His eyes are on the sparrow, and He is aware of every single detail of your life, even the number of hairs on your head (Luke 12:7).

When you can barely hold on any longer, when your faith has weakened, and when you are tempted to feel that God doesn't care or that He can't relate to any of your struggles, always remember this important passage: "For we do not have a high priest who cannot sympathize with our weaknesses, but One who has been tempted in all things just as we are, yet without sin. Therefore let's approach the throne of grace with confidence, so that we may receive mercy and find grace for help at the time of our need" (Hebrews 4:15-16 NASB).

As I reflect on my life–times of laughter and times of crying, times of prosperity and times of drought, times of answered prayers and times of waiting, times of ripe seasons and times of pruning–I realize the Good Gardener was always present.

He is always at work, preparing us for the harvest ahead. His pruning strengthens us, develops our character, teaches us how to persevere, and produces harvest seasons in our lives that we may never experience if we remain unpruned by the Good Gardener.

necessary.

Reflection:

I used to wonder, *If God is present with me, then why would He allow such discomfort at times in my life?* It wasn't until I had children that I realized that sometimes when a good parent is doing what is best for their child, the child may not be aware their parent is making a decision that will protect them or prepare them for maturity.

To this day, now that my kids are adults, there are still times I must watch them grow through their trials and become uncomfortable as they experience pruning processes in their lives. They don't know it hurts me to watch it, especially when I can easily take away their pain. But like a good parent, I am watching. I am near. I love them, and I will do anything to help them as long as it doesn't hinder their growth nor prevent them from maturing so they can later flourish in life.

Sometimes our greatest act of love is not stepping in to take away all the pain, but watching our loved ones grow through it!

I do not claim to have all the answers for every hardship we experience in life. And I certainly do not claim to know why some of us experience a tremendous amount of pain and suffering in our lives. However, I am so grateful God loved me enough to prune me and watch me grow from my place of comfort because it was only in the stretch, the discomfort, the repositioning, and–dare I say–the pain, that produced the greatest harvests in my life!

Recommended Reading:

- *Therefore, since we have been justified through faith, we have peace with God through our Lord Jesus Christ, through whom we have gained access by faith into this grace in which we now stand. And we boast in the hope of the glory of God. Not only so, but we also glory in our sufferings, because we know that suffering produces perseverance; perseverance, character; and character, hope. And hope does not put us to shame, because God's love has been poured out into our hearts through the Holy Spirit, who has been given to us* (Romans 5:1-5 NIV).
- *No discipline seems pleasant at the time, but painful. Later on, however, it produces a harvest of righteousness and peace for those who have been trained by it* (Hebrews 12:11 NIV).
- *For he shall be as a tree planted by the waters, and that spreadeth out her roots by the river, and shall not see when heat cometh, but her leaf shall be green; and shall not be careful in the year of drought, neither shall cease from yielding fruit* (Jeremiah 17:8 KJV).
- *"For I know the plans that I have for you," declares the LORD, "plans for prosperity and not for disaster, to give you a future and a hope"* (Jeremiah 29:11 NASB).

Assignment:

1. As you look back over your life, can you identify times when God was pruning you? How did you feel at that time and how do you feel now?

necessary.

2. Reread John 15:1-2. List examples of "fruit" God has produced in your life as a result of your pruning process.

Chapter 6

Affirmation – Strange Favor

You may not be able to see it right now
Because I am still a work in progress.
But the favor of God is all over my life!

It may not look like favor to you
Because you don't see the expected end.

But just keep watching.

Watch and see what God does.
Watch and see Him turn everything around for my good.

Don't mistake my statement as pride.
And please don't mistake my faith as wishful thinking.

Just keep watching…

And one day you will see
The favor of God has never left me!

[Audio/Video version of this book is available at ZenjaGlass.com]

Chapter 6
Strange Favor

Sometimes favor doesn't look like favor at all!

When my life was falling apart and everything seemed to be spinning out of control, there was no way in the world you could have convinced me that God was showing me favor.

What kind of strange favor is that? How could anyone in their right mind call that favor? Especially when you are going through the storms and don't feel His presence at all.

Favor should come wrapped with pretty bows and fall from the sky, like an angel bringing you a personal delivery from God. Right?

Favor shouldn't look like trouble. Favor shouldn't look like pain or discomfort. Favor shouldn't look like times of uncertainty and attacks from the enemy. Favor shouldn't accompany tears or hardships. That's not favor. Or is it?

Is it possible that this strange favor from God has a greater purpose in our lives that many of us simply cannot see during our storms?

Is it possible that whatever you are going through right now, the strange favor of God is powerfully at work in your life? Moving you. Strengthening you. Making you wiser. Teaching you to persevere. Positioning you for new territory. Taking away what is no longer needed for the next season in your life. Building your character and shaping you to become a light for others. Could it be possible?

necessary.

I am greatly moved by the story of Joseph in the Bible because he went through nearly all the stages I just listed, and at every point the Bible teaches us that the Lord was with him and he was greatly favored by God.

I often asked myself, *How on earth could the Lord be with Joseph and not immediately rescue him from his troubles? How can the Bible teach us the Lord was with him when he was treated so unfairly and endured hardships for years?*

I just couldn't understand how the loving God that we serve could sit with us and wipe away our tears, yet not fix the problem when He has the ability to do so at that very moment. If you love someone, and if you are able to do so, wouldn't you want to immediately take away their pain and discomfort? Those were my thoughts when I was unable to recognize the strange favor God showed Joseph. At first glance, I could not see any favor because it was not wrapped with ribbons and bows. It was wrapped in his suffering!

Let's visit the life of Joseph and explore a biblical example of this strange favor that our Good Father gives us to prepare us for greater blessings and new territory.

I love the story of Joseph in Genesis chapters 37-45 because, not only does his life serve as a blueprint to understanding the strange favor of God, his life also gives a beautiful meaning to the passage: "No weapon that is formed against thee shall prosper" (Isaiah 54:17 KJV). In case you are not familiar with his story, below is a brief recap:

Joseph had a dream that he would reign over his brothers. His brothers hated him and were very angry about that dream. They betrayed Joseph and devised a plot to throw him into a cistern. When they saw Midianite merchants, they pulled him out of the cistern and sold him for 20 shekels of silver to the Ishmaelites. The merchants eventually took Joseph all the way to Egypt, where he was then sold to one of Pharaoh's officials, called Potiphar (Genesis 37).

While in Potiphar's house, "the Lord gave him success in everything he did, Joseph found favor in his eyes and became his attendant. Potiphar put him in charge of his household, and he entrusted to his care everything he owned" (Genesis 39:3-4 NIV). Even though Joseph was stripped away from his family and sold by his own brothers, the Lord gave him success in everything he did. By this point, I would think he has been through enough. God showed him favor despite his family's betrayal. He now had a great job, and in my humble opinion, he should have been left alone to live a happy life. But O' let's examine how God continued to give him more of this strange favor!

Let's see how this strange favor from God was packaged in Joseph's life. If you continue reading Genesis, in chapter 39, you will discover that Joseph was a handsome man and Potiphar's wife was attracted to him. She asked him to sleep with her, but he denied her. Despite her many attempts to seduce him, he refused her because he was an honorable man. So what did she do? She lied and said he tried to sleep with her. By the time you get to verse 20, you will find he was thrown in prison as a result of her lies and betrayal.

How is it possible to have already gone through a traumatic situation, finally gotten settled, and then, without warning, you are unfairly treated and repositioned once again?

That certainly doesn't look like favor to me, yet the Bible tells us, "But while Joseph was there in prison, the LORD was with him; he showed him kindness and granted him FAVOR in the

necessary.

eyes of the prison warden. So the warden put Joseph in charge of all those held in prison" (Genesis 39:20-22 NIV).

What kind of strange favor was that? That favor led him to being betrayed by his family. Favor shouldn't look like family members turning their backs on you. That favor led him to jail. Favor shouldn't look like being blamed for something you didn't do. Right?

I think it's great that God granted Joseph favor with the warden, but he was still in jail against his wishes! Does that look like favor to you? And can you, in any way, relate to this scenario? Let's keep unpacking this strange-looking gift and see what God had inside.

Later, in Genesis 40, while Joseph was in prison he interpreted a dream for another prisoner—the former cupbearer for the king. The cupbearer was very grateful for Joseph's insight. When the cupbearer was later released, Joseph asked that he please remember him. And wouldn't you know it? The cupbearer completely forgot about Joseph!

So let's think about this for a moment. You are already in a place where you have no desire to be. You are betrayed by your family and by a person who lied on you. Then you try to help someone who is in jail with you, and your only request is for them to remember you. But the moment they don't need you anymore, they forget about you. In fact, they went on with their lives and forgot everything you did to help them.

Can anyone relate to this? The powerful part of this season in Joseph's life is that, according to the Bible, even during those times the Lord was with Joseph and granted him favor with others. My God!

Strange Favor

Nearly two years later—yes, two long years—while Joseph was still in jail, Pharaoh had a dream and needed someone to interpret it. But no one was powerful and wise enough to interpret the dream (Genesis 41:8). Then, wouldn't you know it? The cupbearer all of a sudden remembered Joseph and recommended him. Finally, in the Lord's timing might I say, they sent for Joseph to be released from prison to help the king. Surely favor shouldn't look like helping someone, only for them to completely forget about you for years, until they need something from you again. But let's see how Joseph responded.

When asked to interpret his dream, Joseph agreed to help him and, in complete humility, Joseph said, "I cannot do it... but God will give Pharaoh the answer he desires" (Genesis 41:16 NIV). After he interpreted Pharaoh's dream, Pharaoh said, "Since God has made all this known to you, there is no one so discerning and wise as you. You shall be in charge of my palace, and all my people are to submit to your orders... I hereby put you in charge of the whole land of Egypt" (Genesis 41:39-41 NIV).

This has to be a *Selah* moment. We have to take a moment to pause, and just let that soak in!

Do you see how the strange favor of God was at work all along? Joseph went from being in a cistern, to serving a rich governor, to being thrown in jail, then forgotten about for two years, and then in charge of the entire land of Egypt! But the story didn't end there.

There was a severe famine in the land for seven years, and Joseph's brothers ended up in Egypt desperate for food, only to discover that their brother, whom they sold many years earlier, was placed in charge of everything (Genesis 42-44)!

necessary.

My God! This is another *Selah* moment.

We have to pause again and consider this situation. The very people who mistreated him now needed him. How do you think Joseph responded to that?

My heart is greatly touched when I read Genesis 50:18-21 NIV which states, "His brothers then came and threw themselves down before him, 'We are your slaves,' they said. But Joseph said to them, 'Don't be afraid. Am I in the place of God? You intended to harm me, but God intended it for good to accomplish what is now being done, the saving of many lives. So then, don't be afraid. I will provide for you and your children.' And he reassured them and spoke kindly to them."

After Joseph made himself known to his brothers, he not only forgave them, he took care of them and all their children. He also took care of his entire family during the famine and went on to live 110 years! If that is not an example of surrendering to the will of God, then I don't know what is! Joseph clearly understood that, through all the pain, lies, and betrayal, God was working in his favor, to reposition him to later save his family.

My God! That challenges my faith because the kind of love and compassion that Joseph displayed is truly rare nowadays!

When I unfold the events of Joseph's life, I can clearly see the connection between his brothers' mistreating him and Joseph being repositioned in a new land. I can see the connection between Potiphar's wife telling lies, and Joseph going to jail. I can see the hand of God at work by positioning the cupbearer to meet Joseph while in jail. I can see the connection between the cupbearer and Pharaoh so that he could recommend Joseph at the appointed time. I can see the connection between Joseph winning favor in Pharaoh's eyes and eventually becoming second in command of his entire kingdom. I can see how all those events and disheartening circumstances happened to place Joseph in a position of high authority to store up food to survive a seven-year famine. And lastly, I can see how God predestined Joseph to save his family and become a blessing for generations thereafter.

Despite all the betrayals, hardships, slander, jealousy, and envy, Joseph was still highly favored! It is a strange favor that we rarely recognize because it doesn't come wrapped with pretty bows and with angels playing harps in the background. This favor was given to Joseph so that he could be strategically repositioned to not only walk in power, but to save his entire family. Joseph lived 110 years, and three generations after him were blessed with peace and prosperity (Genesis 50:22-23).

How do you think this story would have turned out if Joseph had grown bitter in his heart toward God and refused to help the cupbearer? How would it have turned out if you were in his position throughout all the trials he righteously endured?

I can't help but wonder how my own story would be playing out right now if I refused to allow God to use me through the pain. You will discover later, that even as I write these pages and speak these words, I am going through perhaps the toughest season I have ever experienced in my entire life. But I refuse to reject the strange favor sent from the Lord!

I say this with great conviction: We must be willing to accept the strange favor of God, even when it arrives wrapped in our suffering!

necessary.

Reflection:

Sometimes our blessings are wrapped inside the suffering. And I know it doesn't always seem fair. But I've learned to never reject the strange favor of the Lord. Instead of throwing away my box of pain, I've learned to look at it again, unwrap it, and ask God to show me what's on the inside that can be put to use for His glory.

I won't lie to you. I can't say I am grateful for every difficult thing I ever experienced in life because there were some events when the pain was so great that I wouldn't wish them on anyone. However, I will say this, as I look back over my life, and I reflect on all that God has done, I can truly say the strange favor of the Lord was always upon me.

If you are going through a difficult season right now, I sincerely pray you do not give up. I pray for God to strengthen you, and I pray that you persevere and know that one day, your current season is going to become one of your greatest testimonies!

Stay in the fight my dear brothers and sisters. Stay in the fight! Don't you dare believe the lies of the enemy. Remember, Satan is a masterful liar, the father of lies (John 8:44). God has NOT brought you this far to leave you! His eyes and ears are attentive to your cry (Psalm 34:15).

Jesus [Yeshua] taught us that in this world, we will have trouble (John 16:33). And while this may be difficult to accept, I pray that you find comfort in knowing that our help comes from the Lord. He is watching over you (Psalm 121). He will always provide a way for you to stand up (1 Corinthians 10:13).

Hold on! Though you may not feel His presence... hold on! He is close to the brokenhearted (Psalm 34:18), and He will deliver you from all your troubles (Psalm 34:19).

Strange Favor

Recommended Reading:

I encourage you to read Genesis chapters 37-45 to learn the entire story of Joseph.

Assignment:

1. Can you identify times in your life when you were given strange favor from God? Be specific.

2. As you contemplate the story of Joseph, what lessons have you learned from his story, and how will you apply those lessons to your life now?

[Audio/Video version of this book is available at ZenjaGlass.com]

Chapter 7

Affirmation – God Can Do More with Less

My bank account balance does not get to determine my destiny,

Because God can do so much MORE with LESS!

When He tells me to move forth...

I will move.

Because He provides my provisions along the way!

Therefore, I won't worry about how He is going

To make it happen.

I won't worry about not having enough.

He leads me along green pastures.

He overflows my cup.

He is my Waymaker!

He has never failed me.

And He never will!

[Audio/Video version of this book is available at ZenjaGlass.com]

Chapter 7

God Can Do More with Less

Did you know that God can do more with less? Are you aware that He specializes in doing the impossible?

One of my favorite stories in the Bible is the story of Gideon in the book of Judges, chapters 6 and 7. I love this story because Gideon doubted his ability to save Israel. His clan was the weakest in Manasseh, and he viewed himself as the least in his family (Judges 6:15).

Like many of us, Gideon wasn't certain God would do what He said he would do. Gideon needed signs from God because he just couldn't see how God would show up and do the impossible in his life. Can anyone relate to that?

Can you relate to trusting in God's abilities, but at the same time, not being sure if He will do it for you? I certainly can! But what is so amazing about God is that He understands our weaknesses. In Judges 6:36-40, God honored Gideon's request and gave him a sign that he would be victorious by allowing dew to appear on the wool fleece, on the threshing floor.

But that wasn't enough for Gideon. He needed another sign from God. He said, "'Do not let Your anger burn against me, so that I may speak only one more time; please let me put You to the test only one more time with the fleece: let it now be dry only on the fleece, and let there be dew on all the ground.' And God did so that night; for it was dry only on the fleece, and dew was on all the ground" (Judges 6:39-40 NASB).

necessary.

We can't shake our heads at Gideon, because many of us have done the same thing. There are times when we doubted we heard from the Lord, and we needed another sign from Him to show us that He really was talking to us when He told us to do something of great magnitude. Something well beyond our version of ourselves. Something well beyond our bank account balances. Something well beyond what we think we are capable of accomplishing. Right? Thank God, He was patient with Gideon, and He kept demonstrating His power until Gideon actually believed that, even though he viewed himself as the least (Judges 6:15), he could be victorious with the help of the Lord.

My favorite part of the story of Gideon lies in Judges 7, because God did what no one expected to happen: He strategically began to remove soldiers from Gideon's army. The Lord told Gideon he had too many men to deliver Midian into their hands (Judges 7:2). Keep in mind, according to many Bible scholars, Gideon's army was already considered small, and he was already outnumbered by the people he was about to fight; yet God told him he had too many people.

Now, pause for a minute and ask yourself this question: Why on earth would the Lord reduce Gideon's army from 32,000 men to only 300 men before going into war? That number would have been considered laughable to go against such a vast opposing army.

Does that make any sense to you at all? What was the point of reducing Gideon's army? Why not just let them march into war and give them the victory with the larger version of his army? Why give them LESS to do MORE?

The Lord said to Gideon, "You have too many men. I cannot deliver Midian into their hands, or Israel would boast against me, 'My own strength has saved me.' Now announce to the army, 'anyone who trembles with fear may turn back and leave Mount Gilead.' So, twenty-two thousand men left, while ten thousand remained" (Judges 7:2-3 NIV).

I don't know about you, but when I first read this story, I had to jump out of my chair and pace the floor for a moment because it changed my entire perception of how God is able to move in our lives when we think we are ill-equipped. The Lord made it very clear that He did not want them to think they won the victory by their own strength. My God! He needed for them to know that *He* delivered them... not their own strength or power.

God specializes in doing more with less, and He never sees us as we see ourselves. He sees who we are in *His* presence. Notice when the angel of the Lord first approached Gideon and said, "The LORD is with you, mighty warrior" (Judges 6:12 NIV). I can only imagine Gideon looking around and thinking to himself that surely the angel wasn't talking to him. What mighty warrior? Me?

In fact, his response was, "'Pardon me, my lord,' Gideon replied, 'but if the LORD is with us, why has all this happened to us? Where are all his wonders that our ancestors told us about when they said, "Did not the LORD bring us up out of Egypt?" But now the LORD has abandoned us and given us into the hand of Midian'" (Judges 6:13 NIV).

Can you find yourself in that statement? Do you see how we can sometimes respond to God when we have suffered for a long time? Do you see how Gideon's response was based on his perspective? He questioned God's presence because he could not fathom how God could be with them when they were in dark seasons, enduring long suffering, and considered

necessary.

the least of all. I would be lying to you if I said I couldn't relate to what Gideon was feeling at that moment. There certainly have been times in my life when I wondered where God was and how He could be present when I was going through trials and tribulations.

If you read all of Judges 6 and 7, you will find many gems that you should carry for a lifetime. For me, one of the greatest treasures from this book of the Bible is when I discovered that Gideon did not need more to win the war... he only needed the Lord's STRATEGY!

Let's read verses 16-22 from Judges 7 to see the strategy the Lord gave to Gideon:

"And he divided the three hundred men into three units, and he put trumpets and empty pitchers into the hands of all of them, with torches inside the pitchers. Then he said to them, "Look at me and do likewise. And behold, when I come to the outskirts of the camp, do as I do. When I and all who are with me blow the trumpet, then you also blow the trumpets around the entire camp and say, 'For the Lord and for Gideon!'"

So Gideon and the hundred men who were with him came to the outskirts of the camp at the beginning of the middle night watch, when they had just posted the watch; and they blew the trumpets and smashed the pitchers that were in their hands. When the three units blew the trumpets and broke the pitchers, they held the torches in their left hands and the trumpets in their right hands for blowing, and shouted, "A sword for the Lord and for Gideon!" And each stood in his place around the camp; and all the army ran, crying out as they fled. And when they blew the three hundred trumpets, the Lord set the sword of one against another even throughout the entire army" (Judges 7:16-22 NASB).

Did you catch that? Did you catch what God did? Did you see the strategy God gave Gideon to make his small group of men appear as a mighty force? The Lord caused the opposing men to turn on each other! I wish I had paid closer attention to this story throughout my life, when my resources were dried up and I felt I didn't have enough to make it. I wish I had remembered this when I felt so alone and so afraid because I was uncertain what would become of my future as my life seemed to unravel before my eyes. God can do so much more with less! Gideon was in a situation that most people would agree was impossible to overcome; however, when the hand of the Lord is on our side, and we follow His strategy, we are victorious!

I will never forget when the economy took a major turn many years ago when my kids were young. It seemed as if, almost overnight, my finances plummeted. I was already dealing with some major issues in life, including my marriage and children, and the last thing I wanted to deal with was financial pressures. But I didn't get to choose that season of pruning in my life. It chose me.

So there I was, with a master's degree and many years of experience in the staffing industry as an agency owner, with only a few dollars in my pocket. I started shopping at thrift stores and garage sales, looking for items I could resale online to earn some extra money. Some people looked down on me because they saw who was once a thriving business owner, "scraping for pennies" as one person said to me. It made no sense at all, and nothing I was doing lined up with my career path, but I stayed the course and continued to walk in obedience by doing what God told me to do.

necessary.

Day and night, I worked very hard just to make a little money from reselling items most people would have considered as a waste of time. I can't count the number of days I cried, prayed, and worked into the wee hours of the morning, questioning if I was on the right track. Questioning how I ended up there. Questioning how God could grow anything from something that seemed so little to me. That was an extremely uncomfortable pruning season, and I had absolutely no idea where God was taking me.

But God had a plan all along. He needed to position me so that when He built me back up, I couldn't take pride in my own ability to save myself. He needed to prune me for better use so that I could step out of the box I was secured in and be repositioned for a greater purpose to help others come out of their dark corners.

Looking back at all those years of feeling lost and out of place, I realize God was not punishing me at all. He was uprooting me and nurturing me to become His reflection. So many things were out of order in my life during that time, and I wasn't even aware of the level of pride that hid deep within my heart. Even though I would not have admitted it at the time, I thank God for saving me... from me. His strength is made perfect in weakness (2 Corinthians 12:9) and it was only in my weakness, during some of the most difficult pruning seasons of my life, that I began to let go and surrender into the hands of the Good Gardener.

By His grace, throughout the next few years God took the little bit that I had and turned what was a side job into a viable business and blessed me to expand, employ several people, and help others all over the world. I am absolutely amazed by God's ability to prune with precision to get an expected end.

God Can Do More with Less

All that time when He was allowing my cup to run dry, He was positioning me next to a stream so that I would never thirst again. I am a living witness, God can do so much more with less!

I can't end this chapter without discussing another one of my favorite stories in the Bible—the story of the widow in 2 Kings 4. She was so poor that the creditors were coming to take her two boys as slaves. The prophet Elisha asked her how he could help her. He said, "Tell me, what do you have in your house?" She said, "Your servant has nothing there at all... except a small jar of olive oil" (verse 2). Elisha instructed her to go to all her neighbors and get their empty jars. He then told her, "Don't ask for just a few. Then go inside and shut the door behind you and your sons. Pour oil into all the jars, and as each is filled, put it to one side... They brought the jars to her and she kept pouring" (2 Kings 4:3-5 NIV). Elisha then told her, "Go, sell the oil and pay your debts. You and your sons can live on what is left" (2 Kings 4:7 NIV).

This is an amazing story to me because the widow said she had nothing there at all. She saw her situation as dire. From her viewpoint, she didn't have anything. But the prophet saw potential and opportunities that would be blessed if she was willing to use the tiny bit that she had to pour into empty jars and trust that they would be filled!

I pray the story of the widow and the story of Gideon empowers you to look at your situation again. Sometimes we can view our circumstances and not see anything at all that we can use or do to change our situation. It looks like nothing. Right? It looks like nothing at all. It looks like, "I am not talented enough." It looks like, "I am by myself with no one to help me." It looks like, "Nothing has ever worked out for me,

necessary.

so why would it work this time?" It looks like, "But my dream is too big. I don't have the resources to make that happen."

If you can identify with any of those statements, I humbly ask you, my dear sisters and brothers, look at it again! Look at your situation again through the eyes of God. Ask God what He sees and what He wants you to do with the little bit that you have. Elisha paid no attention to what the poor widow saw in the physical because he was looking in the Spirit. He saw what could be done with just a little bit.

Do you see what God can do with the little bit that you have?

I have found, from my personal experience, sometimes we can't see what is so obvious because we are too close to the problem. And it is only when we go up higher, in the presence of God, that we can view our circumstances from a different angle and see that the little we have is of great value because God can do so much more with less!

Reflection:

I learned so much from my momma when I was a young girl. She could stretch $192 for an entire month to take care of her three kids. I know this because I watched her master it for years. She was skilled at making a pot of beans or a box of spaghetti last for days if needed. And when I think about her life–a young girl from the South whose mother died when she was just a child herself–she accomplished so much with so little. She may never know the lives she has impacted through her children and how generations will be blessed for years to come because she continuously planted the word of God in our hearts and always taught us that God is a Waymaker.

She didn't have much from a worldly perspective, but she showed love to everyone she came into contact with. And when she finally graduated from college (around the same time I graduated from college), she went on to become a social worker to teach, train, and help adults with disabilities, who, to this day, love her so much!

In case you are wondering what this story has to do with this chapter. My answer is... everything!

My momma has everything to do with this chapter because not everything is about making more money or having more resources. She used the little that she had to touch lives everywhere she went. God is able to do so much more with less, in EVERY area of our lives. He is able to multiply and produce fruit that will last, if only we will place the little bit that we have in His hands... and trust the Good Gardener!

Recommending Reading:

I encourage you to read all of Judges 6 and 7.

Assignment:

1. What are your new convictions about God's ability to do more with less?

necessary.

2. Are you willing to learn from the story of the widow's oil and look at your circumstances again? If so, please spend some time in prayer and ask God to show you what He sees with the little bit that you have. What do you now see?

Chapter 8

Affirmation – Is It Mine?

It Is Mine!

God said it is mine...

So, I shall have it!

And what He reveals in the Spirit

Must manifest in the physical!

How can I be so certain of these promises I cannot see?

How can I walk with confidence knowing that it will come to be?

Because He has never lied

And He never will!

When He tells me it is mine,

I shall have it!

Nothing will keep me from holding in my hands

What has been given to me by my Father.

When God says it is mine...

I shall have it indeed!

[Audio/Video version of this book is available at ZenjaGlass.com]

Chapter 8

Is It Mine?

When God says it is yours, it is yours! Period.

The question is, are you then willing to go get it?

One of the most important spiritual revelations I have learned is to capture in the Spirit what belongs to me before I attempt to get it in the physical.

It took me nearly 30 years of reading and studying my bible before I understood that everything must be attained in the Spirit before it is manifested in the physical. I had no idea that the spiritual forces of evil in the heavenly realms were a real force, and there is a real battle that we must be aware of (Ephesians 6:12). And I certainly had no idea that as children of the Most High God, we can join Him in the Spirit and walk in the dominion, power, and authority God gave us (Genesis 1:26, Psalm 8:6-8, Revelation 1:6), and command the earth to yield what God says is ours! Not only that, but we can stand in authority and force spiritual wickedness in high places to flee (James 4:7) and submit to the word of God concerning our lives, His purpose for us, His provisions, His protection, and much more.

I know that may be a bit heavy to digest at one time, but I would be doing a great disservice to God if I left this important chapter out of this book because this revelation has changed my entire life! I posted four video podcast episodes on this topic, called, "Get It Before You Get It." This can be accessed

necessary.

on my website at www.ZenjaGlass.com. I will do my best to summarize all four sessions in this chapter so that you can capture the essence of this process.

There are four processes I tend to go through before I make any major commitments to achieve something of great magnitude. I learned this from simply studying Bible principles, as I became aware this was the process God continued to walk me through. This process keeps me from second-guessing myself. It also helps me stay in the fight when opposition arises as I walk in alignment with what God has told me to do.

Before I attempt to attain anything in the physical, I first have to be reminded of who God says I am. Second, I have to know if it is the Lord's will for me to have what I am requesting or what He has shown me. Third, I have to actually become that person who has ALREADY received it. And lastly, I have to take action to get or receive what God has shown is mine.

Who am I? That is the first question I ask myself when I am facing a huge mountain, or perhaps a challenging goal or opportunity that seems impossible for me to become, receive, or acquire. I have to spend time in the presence of my Father to be reminded of who He says I am. And sometimes this takes days, weeks, months, or even years, before He has molded me enough for me to believe in who He says I am. When I know who I am, and I see my Father's reflection when I look in the mirror, I have the courage of a mighty lion and a level of faith in doing the impossible that I cannot attain on my own. So for me, the first step is that I have to know I am a child of God. I have to be reminded that I am a royal priest (1 Peter 2:9-10), an ambassador for Christ (2 Corinthians 5:20), an heir of God and a co-heir with Jesus Christ (Romans 8:17), and as an heir

Is It Mine?

with Jesus Christ, a seed of Abraham and heir of his promises (Galatians 3:29). I must remember my Father has all authority in heaven and on earth (Matthew 28:18). And I must know that I did not receive a Spirit that makes me a slave to fear (Romans 8:15), but I have been given power, dominion, and authority by my Father (John 14:12-14, Romans 8:11, Revelation 5:10).

Consider the question Moses asked after speaking to the Lord in the burning bush on Mount Horeb. When Moses was told to go to Pharaoh, one of the most powerful men on the earth, and command him to let His people go, Moses asked the most important question that was needed, "'Who am I that I should go to Pharaoh and bring the Israelites out of Egypt?' And God said, 'I will be with you.' Then Moses said, 'Suppose I go to the Israelites and say to them, "The God of your fathers has sent me to you," and they ask me, "What is his name?" Then what shall I tell them?' God said to Moses, 'I AM WHO I AM. This is what you are to say to the Israelites: I AM has sent me to you.'" (Exodus 3:11-14 NIV).

Did you catch that? Did you catch that Moses was not sure who he was, as many of us may feel when God gives us a dream or a task so large that we question, "Who am I, that I should be able to accomplish this?" Did you also catch that Moses needed to know who sent him? He needed to know by what authority they should obey his request. This is one of the primary secrets to success that you should never forget: Before you begin your journey, you must know who you are and, just as importantly, who sent you!

Once God has reminded me who I am in His presence, and I am confident He is sending me, I begin the next process by asking, "Lord, is it mine?" This is when I spend time in His

necessary.

presence and get a visual in my Spirit of what He says I shall have. I need His assurance that I am walking in alignment with what He wants me to do. I value this time as I sit with Him and get a very detailed vision of exactly what He says is mine.

You may recall, before King David overtook the Amalekites, he asked the Lord, "Shall I pursue after this troop? Shall I overtake them? And he answered him, Pursue: for thou shalt surely overtake them, and without fail recover all" (1 Samuel 30:8 KJV).

Why do you think David sought an answer from the Lord BEFORE going into battle? In my humble opinion, it is because he needed to know, "Is it mine? Shall I go get what you have already granted to me?" I don't know about you, but I tend to walk with a lot more confidence when I go into a situation knowing God has already taken care of it.

It is so important that we seek counsel from God before attempting to do anything important in our lives. Because once we know that God has validated and confirmed what we are to do, or what we are to receive, there is no devil in hell that can stop us or change our course. Why? Because we will walk in confidence, knowing God sent us. And what He says is ours, we shall have!

As long as we know we were sent from our Father to receive what He has already shown us in the Spirit, we are able to withstand and overcome the obstacles and roadblocks the enemy tries to place in our paths to discourage us. Nothing can take away what our Father has already GIVEN us in Christ, "in whom are hidden all the treasures of wisdom and knowledge" (Colossians 2:2-3 NIV).

Is It Mine?

As a practical example, this reminds me of a time in my life when I had to give a presentation for a major account with my new startup company many years ago. It was one of the largest corporations in the country. I remember driving around their headquarters many times, praying to God to reveal to me if it is mine. I drove around their parking lot, claiming it in the Spirit, and God revealed to me, it shall be my account.

I will never forget the day I walked into their conference room, probably one of the largest conference rooms I'd ever seen. It was filled with senior-level executives and almost every major competitor I could think of. They arrived in teams and carried briefcases, wore tailored suits, and gave fancy presentations with beautiful charts and displays. And there I was, walking through the door with no one but God by my side. Just before I entered the room, a lady said to me, "Don't be intimidated. There are a lot of people here." And I responded, "Oh, I am not intimidated at all. I am ready!"

It wasn't pride speaking, it was the confidence that came from getting it in the Spirit first. I was simply there to receive it! I knew that God had already delivered that client into my hands, and I just simply needed to go and get it. I was so incredibly comfortable when I presented my company to all their shareholders and executives that I walked around the room as I gave my presentation and spoke to them as if I were having an annual meeting with my own staff.

By the time my presentation concluded, one of their directors greeted me and said, "You are exactly what we have been looking for." By the grace of God, even though the odds were greatly stacked against me, I was awarded the account! I

necessary.

couldn't thank God enough for giving me what He told me was mine!

The third process I experience before receiving what is mine in the physical is to BECOME the person God has shown me. I literally walk, talk, think, and take action as if I am already that person... that higher version of myself that God has called me to become.

For example, I remember telling my friends that I am going to write a bestselling book that is going to help many people draw nearer to God from all over the world. I made that a natural part of my conversation. So instead of saying, "I can't spend time with you this weekend," I would say, "I can't get together this weekend. I am still writing a bestseller that is going to change hearts all over the nation, and draw people closer to God." It wasn't arrogance speaking. It was me becoming who God showed me I would become.

As I type and read these pages right now, I have not sold a single copy of my book, but God has already shown me in the Spirit that this book, His book might I add, will spread to all nations, help prevent suicides, encourage hearts, transform mindsets, inspire people to pursue their dreams, and move hearts closer to Him. I received it. I claim it. And right now, in real time, I am becoming that person who has written a best-selling book that will impact nations!

During this third step of the process, I believe it is also very important to write or record a detailed affirmation for yourself from the viewpoint of the person you have become. Write this affirmation and read it (or play it) aloud on a daily basis to transform your mindset and remind your spirit of the direction you are heading. You will notice that you will start making decisions and plans that align with your renewed self. When I read my affirmation, or listen to my recording, I recite it so that the earth can hear and send for my helpers to come forth. Yes, God sends helpers and grants us to have favor with people as we walk in alignment (Psalm 5:12, Psalm 84:11, Proverbs 3:4). I also recite it to put the enemy on notice so that his flaming arrows are returned, because I am shielded by God's protection (Psalm 3:3).

God confirmed I would help millions of people come to know Him. He confirmed some people will avoid committing suicide because they heard my podcast or read my book. He confirmed I will give to those in need, serve as a light to pull people out of dark places, help more kids with chronic medical conditions, and help fund the rescue of even more children who are victims of human trafficking. He confirmed my finances will be in order and my company will have organizational structure and operate in love, dignity, honesty, and respect. He confirmed that, though I do not hold any ministry licenses issued by men, nor do I oversee a church, He will use me to spread His word to all nations. And I believe Him!

I speak this daily over my life. I am simply an instrument He is using. Each time I write a chapter, I ask Him to set my fingers on fire with His Holy Spirit and simply write through me into the hearts of people to draw them closer to Him. It has taken years to finally release this book, but I keep telling God it is His book, not mine. I will only write what and when He tells me to write because I am on His assignment.

The fourth step that I take in this process is actually getting or receiving what God has shown me in the Spirit. If I know who I am, if God has confirmed what is mine, and I walk in faith as I become that greater version of myself, then I must take

necessary.

action and simply go and get what He ALREADY gave me. Allow me to give another practical example.

I remember when God told me it was time to launch my agency, and though I had very little money and was going through a very rough time in life, I knew I needed to walk in obedience. I rented an office space and started buying used furniture for my reception lounge and for my interviewing room. I didn't have a single client and no money to hire a single person, but God spoke to me so clearly; and because we spent so much time together, I knew the sound of His voice. I knew to run immediately in obedience and do what He said!

As soon as I acquired the space and furnished my office, I received a call from an old associate of mine and she became my first client! Within a week or so, another client came on board, and I simply fell to my knees in gratitude to God for sending my helpers and sustaining me. I am beyond grateful to God for protecting His integrity and for opening doors I could not see with physical eyes.

If you are feeling discouraged because you were doing your best to walk in faith and things did not work out, I have something to tell you. You are not alone. Keep going! It happens to all of us. Sometimes, I did exactly what God told me to do, and it still didn't work out. Those moments used to really discourage me because it made me question if I really heard from Him in the first place. It also made me question if I was talented enough to achieve what He had in mind. Those were very confusing and discouraging times, but now I realize God didn't make any mistakes at all. It is only in hindsight that I am now able to see: Every single event I once referred to as a failure was actually a setup for my success because I learned a lot along the way and grew quite a bit through all the setbacks. That is a key part to how I am able to move forward now. Things are not perfect in my life. I still have challenges. I still have to deal with issues and pivot and make changes as I grow. But I am grateful for all I have learned along the way and the person God has shaped me to become throughout the process.

For this reason, we should not be quick to turn around when opposition presents itself. That is the time to dig through our toolbox of past trials and find the tools we need to build a different bridge and continue moving forward. I don't know what I would do if my toolbox was empty! I would be completely messed up right now had I not experienced all those past failures and learned from them. There are so many areas of my life where I would have made major mistakes by reacting in a panic when opposition presented itself. I would have easily taken the wrong advice or gone down the wrong path if I did not have previous experience to draw from, and the wisdom from God to navigate my journey.

In fact, just the other day, someone said to me that he is so grateful for our failures and setbacks because if we did not learn from the mistakes we made in the past, we would not be able to avoid the many pitfalls that once held us back. I find it very interesting that all our past failures serve a valuable purpose because at least we know what NOT to do! Everything we have experienced can be used to our benefit and to the glory of God. God has plans to prosper us and not to harm us (Jeremiah 29:11). I pray this has greatly encouraged you.

I don't want to end this chapter without addressing a common question people ask on my podcast when I discuss this topic in greater detail. The question is: "How do you really know if you are hearing from God?"

necessary.

To be clear, I am just a woman who loves God and is doing my very best to use my life experiences to help others and tell the world about Him. So I will answer this question to the best of my knowledge, based on my experience. There are four measures that help me determine if I am truly hearing from God.

1. God will never contradict His word. What I hear must line up with the scriptures.
2. He often reveals things I have not thought of doing. Many times it challenges me, such as starting a podcast to encourage people, even though I did not like social media at all.
3. He won't let up. When God is adamant about me doing something, He keeps reminding me or He keeps allowing doors to close until I walk in step with Him.
4. Whenever He tells me to do something, it always involves a level of service in some way to help others.

While this may not be a foolproof system to know when God is speaking to you, it has certainly helped me to walk in peace and in confidence when I believe He has spoken to me. And, of course, I've made mistakes along the way, primarily by trying to run ahead of Him and do what I think is best. But our loving Father always has a way of rescuing us, humbling us, and getting us back on track as we seek to do His will.

May we love God with all our heart, mind, body, and soul. And one day, may we all hear Him say to us, "Well done, good and faithful servant!" (Matthew 25:21 NIV).

Is It Mine?

Reflection:

Over the years, I have upset a few people who were waiting on an answer from me because they could not understand that I was still waiting on an answer from God. But I have learned the hard way, to wait for God to reveal what is mine in the Spirit before I attempt to grab it in the physical. It is not time wasted, because I have found that receiving what is for me in the Spirit BEFORE attempting to get it in the physical has saved me years of pain and frustration.

Recommended Reading:

- *For all who are led by the Spirit of God are sons of God* (Romans 8:14 ESV).
- *"They said to him, 'Please inquire of God to learn whether our journey will be successful.' The priest answered them, 'Go in peace. Your journey has the LORD'S approval.'"* (Judges 18:5-6 NIV).
- *David inquired of the LORD, "Shall I go up into any of the cities of Judah?" And the LORD said to him, "Go up." David said, "To which shall I go up?" And he said, "To Hebron."* (2 Samuel 2:1 ESV).
- *The people of Israel arose and went up to Bethel and inquired of God, "Who shall go up first for us to fight against the people of Benjamin?" And the LORD said, "Judah shall go up first."* (Judges 20:18 ESV).
- *For the LORD gives wisdom; from his mouth come knowledge and understanding* (Proverbs 2:6 ESV).
- *When the Spirit of truth comes, he will guide you into all the truth, for he will not speak on his own authority,*

necessary.

> *but whatever he hears he will speak, and he will declare to you the things that are to come. He will glorify me, for he will take what is mine and declare it to you. All that the Father has is mine; therefore I said that he will take what is mine and declare it to you* (John 16:13-15 ESV).

- *How much better is it to get wisdom than gold! And to get understanding rather to be chosen than silver!* (Proverbs 16:16 KJV).
- *For to the one who pleases him God has given wisdom and knowledge and joy* (Ecclesiastes 2:26 ESV).
- *Do not be conformed to this world, but be transformed by the renewal of your mind, that by testing you may discern what is the will of God, what is good and acceptable and perfect* (Romans 12:2 ESV).

Assignment:

I encourage you to spend time in your secret place with God as long as needed until He reveals to you who you are and what is yours.

I challenge you to write or record your own affirmation page from the point of view of the person you are BECOMING. Pray about this daily and read it aloud each day as you walk in expectation to receive what God has shown you.

Chapter 9

Affirmation – Open Your Eyes!

All that time

My eyes were closed.

I was fighting battles that had already been won...

And I didn't even know it.

I didn't know the real fight was won in the Spirit

Before my earthly battles even began!

But now, my eyes are open

And I can finally see

The army of God was always with me!

Thank you God for opening my eyes!

Thank you for making me victorious!

[Audio/Video version of this book is available at ZenjaGlass.com]

Chapter 9

Open Your Eyes!

Can you imagine for a moment if we lived each day with our eyes opened?

I can't help but wonder how radically different our lives would be if our spiritual eyes were open and we saw not only the enemy at work, but the mighty hand of God at work as well. I wonder if we would continue doing some of the things we do if we could see the Holy Spirit grieving when we go against the commands of God (Ephesians 4:30).

Would our prayer life be radically different because we could see what happens in the Spirit when we pray? Would we love each other more because we could see the flaming arrows that were sent to produce discord and hatred? I wonder if we would worry about anything at all because we could see the army of God all around us… we could see that the battles we face have already been won (Psalm 34:7).

One of my favorite stores in the Bible is the story of the prophet Elisha in 2 Kings 6. The King of Aram sent horses and chariots and a strong force to surround his home to capture him. When Elisha's servant got up the next morning and saw they were surrounded by the king's army, the servant said, "Oh no, my lord! What shall we do?" (2 Kings 6:15 NIV).

Elisha's response is something I will never forget. He said to his servant, "Don't be afraid… Those who are with us are more than those who are with them." He went on to say, "'Open his eyes, LORD, so that he may see.' Then the LORD opened the servant's

necessary.

eyes, and he looked and saw the hills full of horses and chariots of fire all around Elisha. As the enemy came down toward him, Elisha prayed to the LORD, 'Strike this army with blindness.' So he struck them with blindness, as Elisha had asked" (2 Kings 6:16-18 NIV).

This is a *Selah* moment. We have to pause and take a break to think about this story.

You would think Elisha would have prayed for his enemies to be destroyed or perhaps asked God to send His angels to carry him and his servant away. Isn't that what we do all the time? We ask God to take it all away. But that is not what the prophet Elisha prayed for. Instead, Elisha simply prayed to the Lord to open his eyes!

Elisha was confident of God's protection. It didn't matter that he seemed outnumbered and an entire army was against him. It didn't matter that he had no physical weapons to fight with. It didn't matter, because his eyes were opened... and he knew the Lord was with him.

Can you imagine if we really believed the angel of the Lord encamped around us as stated in Psalm 34:7?

How would we view our situations and circumstances if we lived our lives with unshakable faith and confidence because we know that the true battles we face are not against flesh and blood, but in the spiritual realms (Ephesians 6:12)?

I can only imagine the amount of peace and joy we would experience if our spiritual eyes were wide open and we really believed the passage that states: "He who is in you is greater than he who is in the world." (1 John 4:4 ESV).

When faced with opposition and all odds seemed to be stacked against them, Elisha prayed for his servant's eyes to be open.

Why is that? Were they closed before? And when we look at what opposes us, and all the challenges that come our way, are our eyes closed?

Can you imagine how the servant must have felt when his eyes were opened and he saw the hills full of horses and chariots of fire all around Elisha? If I were there, I am sure I would have thought, "All this time I was worrying for nothing. I had nothing to be afraid of because the army of God was encamped around us this entire time!"

Sometimes we can be too close to the issues we are worried about and they seem insurmountable. We can become so worried about the magnitude of the problem that we convince ourselves we are stuck, because we see no way out. And we all know what comes after that. The enemy begins to feed us statements such as: "You should be further along in life at this point. You are a failure. There is no way to get out of this situation. You are stuck."

When our spiritual eyes are closed, fear can keep us in bondage. Fear of what could happen. Fear of being alone. Fear of not being accepted. Fear of failure. And for some, fear of succeeding. But God did not give us a spirit of fear. He gave us a spirit of sonship (Romans 8:15). When our eyes are closed, our problems seem to magnify and fear begins to creep in when we can't figure out the solution. If we are not aware of what is truly happening, we can find ourselves relying on our own strength and becoming afraid, as Elisha's servant did. His spiritual eyes were not open. He didn't see the presence of God, and like many of us, he began to worry.

I have to mention a situation that happened to me many years ago when I thought I lost everything as I was just getting my new small business off the ground. My podcast episode #30 "My Testimony- Part 1" details the entire story, along with a guest speaker who witnessed it all. I used all my money to invest in

necessary.

some products I was selling online. God made it clear to me that I would have a harvest if I walked in obedience. However, just before the holidays, my products were placed in recall by my primary vendor because one of the units in my bundle was recalled by the supplier. I was devastated! I had thousands of units ready to sell, and with no warning, I was in jeopardy of losing it all. I had nothing to fall back on, and words can't explain the fear that overwhelmed me.

As I was returning a few of my remaining items back to the supplier, I prayed to God for help, and asked Him to open my eyes. He reminded me that He did not give me a spirit of fear, but a spirit of power (2 Timothy 1:7). And just as I was returning a few items, with tears in my eyes because I thought I had lost everything, God told me to stop and purchase even more inventory with the little money I had left. I was literally in front of the supplier, returning a few items, and I said, "I changed my mind. I am keeping them... and buying MORE."

You have to understand, that decision made no sense whatsoever because I already had thousands of units in recall, and the holiday season was only a few days away. So why on earth would I use the little money I had left to go buy more inventory that would be rejected by my primary vendor? You can listen to that podcast episode to hear the entire story, but the shortest version is, I walked in obedience and did what God said because He told me in the Spirit what was mine!

Just before the holiday season ended, we realized the primary vendor made a mistake and our product was not in recall. As soon as we notified them of the error, they placed our listings as active, and we sold out in about two days! As it turned out, we were one of few vendors who continued to stock supplies at the last minute; therefore, when demand was at its highest, we had the stock to meet the need. I am so grateful God opened my eyes and showed me that things were not what they appeared to be.

Open Your Eyes!

In fear, I saw only my problems in front of me, and I almost gave up; but God opened my eyes to see who surrounded my problems. In one day, God took me from nearly going out of business, to having my most productive season, by simply opening my eyes!

To God be all the glory!

The Bible teaches us that God always provides a way out (1 Corinthians 10:13); however, when our eyes are closed, we may not see it. This is why we must develop an intimate relationship with God and pray continuously so that our spiritual eyes can be open and we can be alert and aware of the devil's schemes (1 Peter 5:8). When our spiritual eyes are opened, we get to shift the entire atmosphere by forcing our fears and our problems to turn around... and notice who is present!

Take a moment and think about how you would feel right now if the Lord opened your eyes and you saw the mighty hand of God and His protection in your life at this very moment? How would you react to situations you are worried about if you could see the solution surrounding your problem?

Just imagine for a moment if you could see the army of God encamping around you. What would that do to your confidence?

Imagine if your eyes were opened and you really believed Psalm 91:11 (ESV): "For he will command his angels concerning you to guard you in all your ways."

Imagine if you took Jesus for His word when He said, "Truly, truly, I say to you, whoever believes in me will also do the works that I do; and greater works than these will he do, because I am going to the Father" (John 14:12 ESV).

Can you imagine if you really lived each day with your spiritual eyes opened... and actually believed that?

necessary.

This is the confidence I sincerely pray we all have in God one day. And I won't pretend to act as if I have completely arrived. I won't pretend as if I walk around all day, every day, with my spiritual eyes opened.

Sometimes, I simply forget who I am and the power that resides inside of me. And sometimes I get afraid. Sometimes I forget the real battle is fought in the Spirit. And it is only when I have worried too long about a situation that I realize my eyes were closed the entire time.

That is when I run back to my secret hiding place with my Father, and I say to Him, "Father, remind me again of who I am in your presence. I am sorry I forgot. Tell me again, who am I?"

Then, I kneel before God, with tears running down my face as He gently reminds me that I am His child, a lion, a co-heir (Romans 8:17), and I have tremendous power living inside of me to overcome anything the world can send my way!

I believe we should always ask God to open our eyes so that we can see what He sees. Because when He opens our eyes, nothing will look the same. Our problems will suddenly become opportunities to grow. What stands in our way will become our leverage to go higher. And what once gripped us in fear, will no longer have a hold on us.

When we stand in the power, and in the authority given to us in the name of Jesus Christ [Yeshua], no devil in hell can claim any access to us! When our eyes are opened, every problem, every challenge, and every negative thought has to shift to a higher level, where it must bow down in the secret place, in the presence of God.

This is the power we all must walk in. When we stand with our Father, we don't run from our problems; we tell our problems where to run!

Open Your Eyes!

Reflection:

I can't explain the peace that I feel when my spiritual eyes are opened. It's as if I can feel God's presence all around me, and despite what is occurring before my physical eyes, my soul finds rest in God alone (Psalm 62:1) because I know who watches over me.

This is why we must run to our secret place as often as we can. My prayer is for all of us to develop an intimate relationship with the Lord. And I pray that our bond with Him is so tight and so trustworthy that, no matter who or what comes our way, we know God is with us because our eyes are open!

Recommended Reading:

- *The LORD is my light and my salvation; whom shall I fear? The LORD is the stronghold of my life; of whom shall I be afraid?... Though an army encamp against me, my heart shall not fear; though war arise against me, yet I will be confident (Psalm 27:1-3 ESV).*
- *The angel of the LORD encamps around those who fear Him, and rescues them (Psalm 34:7 NASB).*

Assignment:

1. Spend at least 5-10 minutes with your eyes closed, and just imagine God's protection all around you. What do you see, and how does it make you feel?

necessary.

2. What have you learned from Elisha when he faced opposition? How will you apply this to your life when you face challenges?

Chapter 10

Affirmation – Hidden

A Message to God:

All that time I thought you were punishing me
Because you kept me hidden

Out of sight
Frustrated by my own efforts,
And discouraged by countless setbacks and delays.

But now the time has come.
Now it all makes sense.

You loved me enough to hide me.
To mold me.

To protect me from what I could not see.
To move people out of my way.
To shield me from the enemy.

Thank you for hiding me
Until the timing was right for Your glory to be revealed in me.

Thank you for hiding me.
Until I became your reflection!

[Audio/Video version of this book is available at ZenjaGlass.com]

Chapter 10
Hidden

I believe there are times in our lives when God hides us because He loves us. And I know it doesn't always feel like love. It feels like we are being punished... left behind... and forgotten. After all, if He loves us, why would He allow our prayers and dreams to be delayed for so long? Right?

I know it looks like punishment, but will you consider that perhaps God is simply protecting you, developing you, and calling you to draw nearer to Him in the secret place? He knows what we need before we move to higher levels. He knows the spiritual muscles we must develop. And it is my personal conviction that sometimes He hides us until we are ready to be revealed to the world for His glory.

Most of us don't like waiting, especially when we feel we have waited long enough. We ask God, "When will it be my turn? When will you bring the dream you gave me to a reality? Why do I have to go through so much, and wait so long for you to grant what I've been praying for?"

If you've ever experienced long seasons of crying out for answers, working hard for years with little to no results, or begging God to open doors, only to see them remain closed, I pray this chapter will greatly encourage you.

God hid me for many years. I endured long seasons of not seeing the results I wanted, while He kept me hidden. I am so grateful He did not give me what I wanted when I thought I was ready for it. There were so many things that needed to change in my life, but I didn't see it at the time. I only focused on what I wanted, and not on who I needed to become.

necessary.

It is only in hindsight that I now realize, what I was searching for, was always searching for me. But I needed to grow and become a higher version of myself, not only to receive, but to maintain what God had in store for me. I also needed to learn how to wait on Him without getting frustrated or discouraged.

I am reminded of a passage that helped me during some of the darkest seasons of my life when I thought I couldn't go another day if God didn't step in and change my situation. It states:

"Do not be anxious about anything, but in everything by prayer and pleading with thanksgiving let your requests be made known to God. And the peace of God, which surpasses all comprehension, will guard your hearts and minds in Christ Jesus" (Philippians 4:6-7 NASB).

Can you imagine what could have happened if Ruth left Naomi, took matters into her own hands, and missed the opportunity to marry Boaz, which led to the birth of King David (Ruth 1-4)? This is why waiting on the timing of God is of the utmost importance when we grow weary as we wait for God to make a move.

If you want exposure in your life and you seek to influence people all over the world, the best thing you can do is run and hide with God! You don't have to worry about how to gain attention from others because when God pours His wisdom into you, and you begin to walk in alignment with His timing and His purpose for your life, nations will be drawn to you!

They won't have any choice but to search and find you because the timing and favor of God over your life will show you as the solution to their problems. You will become a city on a hill that cannot be hidden (Matthew 5:14)! When you embrace hiding in the presence of God, may "your light shine before others, so that they may see your good works and give glory to your Father who is in heaven" (Matthew 5:16 ESV).

As a mother of four children, I understand the pressures that come with doing your best to take care of your family while waiting on God to show up and make a way out of no way. And I understand how scary it can be when He seems to remain silent. But I have learned, even in His silence, He is moving! And when He hides us, He is working it out. God's timing and His strategy can change our entire economy in one day (2 Kings 7, Genesis 41:39-43). He is able to give us riches stored in secret places (Isaiah 45:3, Psalm 112:3), bring peace and position us for greatness (Psalm 1:3, Proverbs 3:1-2, Daniel 2:21), and reveal wisdom and strategies in the hidden places (Judges 7:13-22, Daniel 2:22) that can make us victorious and position us to bless others for generations to come!

Let us not forget about the example set for us in Matthew 17:24-27 when Peter went to Jesus to discuss paying the temple tax. Without hesitation, Jesus told him that there would be a drachma coin in the mouth of the first fish Peter would catch. He then instructed Peter to go to the lake, catch that fish, open its mouth, and use that coin to pay their taxes.

Do you think Jesus was worried about money at all? Did He not know where to instruct Peter to go to solve the issue? It's amazing how we forget this at times. Instead of hiding away with God, where secrets are revealed, we run ahead in search of our own coins, while God has all the strategies we will ever need!

I am a living witness that when you spend time hiding in the secret place, He not only whispers His strategies (which many times challenges us to think on higher levels), but He also reveals hidden treasures and makes people show us favor

necessary.

because His wisdom is supreme (Proverbs 3:4, Proverbs 4:7). In fact, the Bible teaches us, "Wisdom is more precious than rubies, and nothing you desire can compare with her" (Proverbs 8:11 NIV).

King David was hidden for many years. Did you know that young David was not even initially considered when the prophet Samuel went to the house of Jesse of Bethlehem to anoint one of his sons to be King over Israel (1 Samuel 16:1-13)? David was still in the fields, tending the sheep while the prophet met his brothers. Think about all those years God hid David while he tended sheep, played the lyre, mastered the use of a slingshot to protect the sheep from the lions and bears, and grew in his intimacy with God. Have you considered, none of those years were wasted? When it was time for David to defeat Goliath, he was ready! And at the proper time, he became King!

I love what David told Saul in 1 Samuel 17:34-37 KJV. He said, "Thy servant kept his father's sheep, and there came a lion, and a bear, and took a lamb out of the flock… The LORD that delivered me out of the paw of the lion, and out of the paw of the bear, he will deliver me out of the hand of this Philistine."

All that time, when David was being hidden, protecting the sheep, playing the lyre (1 Samuel 16:18-23), taking lunch to his brothers as they fought on the battlefield (1 Samuel 17:17-19), and being overlooked by his family (1 Samuel 16:8-13), he was growing and being prepared to become King!

This is a *Selah* moment. This is a moment you should take some time to pause and reflect on this story and consider what God may be developing in you during your season of being hidden, and dare I say… your season of being trained. If you take the time to think about David's journey, you will discover, there was nothing that he went through that was wasted. All of it was necessary for the appointed time!

As a side note, I tried writing other books in the past, and nothing really came of them. I wrote them on my own efforts, and all I had in mind was making money from them. I wrote two career books, and even after getting national exposure, nothing much came of them. I also wrote some books I had little to no interest in, simply because a friend suggested it. This entire story is detailed in my podcast episode #002 "Stop Chasing Seeds." I tell you this story so that you can learn from my mistakes. Instead of dwelling in the secret place with my Father in heaven, I was too busy running around, chasing seeds that God did not plant inside of me, just to make a few dollars. I have learned the hard way–God's plan, His timing, and His strategy will always triumph over mine!

Yes, I still mess up and try to run ahead of Him at times. And no, I still don't like waiting, but I've learned, not all open doors were meant for me to enter. Satan knows how to open doors as well! For this reason, I have learned to be a little bit more patient because, "With the Lord a day is like a thousand years, and a thousand years are like a day. The Lord is not slow in keeping His promise, as some understand slowness. Instead he is patient with you, not wanting anyone to perish, but everyone to come to repentance" (2 Peter 3:8-9 NIV).

Sometimes we may not realize when we ask for something, we are really asking for more pressure. Running a business is a lot of pressure. Influencing others and leading by example is a lot of pressure. Raising a family is a lot of pressure. Buying a home is a lot of pressure. And each time a new door opens, a level of responsibility comes with it. This is why we must remember, when God slows us down and hides us, we must use that time to dwell deeper with Him so that we can mature, gain discernment, and get prepared for what's waiting on us.

necessary.

We must learn to trust that God knows when we need to be hidden long enough to develop the spiritual muscles and the integrity to handle the level of PRESSURE we have requested.

I am convinced, without a shadow of a doubt, that I would have caused tremendous damage and made irreversible mistakes in my life, had God given me everything that I wanted, when I wanted it. I couldn't handle what I was praying for at that time because that lower version of myself lacked discipline, spiritual discernment, and intimacy with God.

My pride alone would have ruined everything. And, of course, at the time I would have never admitted it, but I was nowhere near capable of handling not only the pressures but the blessings I was asking for at that time in my life. I know me enough to know that I would have completely skipped the lessons on compassion, humility, and worldliness if God had given me what I thought I needed at that moment. I cried and pleaded with God, and kicked and yelled, and screamed and prayed, and did some of everything to get His attention, but all He would do was hide me!

He hid me from myself to keep me from destroying myself. My God! I am so grateful!

God had to humble me in ways that rocked me to my core so that He could build me back up and use me for His good will. There are so many lessons I learned along the way that now anchor me and sustain me in life.

I am finally learning to appreciate the seasons when He hides me. They are not always desirable, but highly valued because His wisdom transforms my life, and His divine protection keeps me from striking my foot against a stone (Psalm 91:11-12). Because He loves me, He hides me.

I know it's uncomfortable to wait on God, especially when you need answers, but I plead with you to never allow your frustrations to be used as weapons against yourself by running ahead of Him. Accept His open invitation, and hide with Him.

Many years ago, when I was so discouraged by all the setbacks in my life, I finally made the decision to stop trying to force things to happen, and wait on God to move. I expected to gain peace in my heart, but I didn't expect for God to reveal His secrets to me. I didn't expect to actually catch His attention!

This very book you are reading or listening to is a prime example of His strategy at work in the secret places. I will never forget, many years ago, when God woke me up in the middle of the night and whispered to me that I would write a book and call it, "necessary." When I saw the vision of the book, my name wasn't on the cover page, it was just the word "necessary" that I saw in the secret place. He told me that is exactly how it will look. I had no idea that, many years later, He would actually manifest it to happen in my life.

A good friend of mine who serves as a business consultant once reminded me that the true measure of success is doing what God tells us to do, in the time He allows. That is important advice to treasure, and I pray we never forget it.

Success is not always based on tangible items or even dreams fulfilled. It has little to do with what we can hold in our hands or brag about. True success is walking under the mantle of favor that God gives us, as we live our lives in ways that influence others to seek Him. When people want to know who God is and what He is capable of doing, they should be able to look at our lives as a living testimony.

necessary.

In my humble opinion, no man is rich if he is not rich in honoring God in his life. I don't care about how good you look, how much money you have in your account, what senior-level position you hold, or how beautiful your home is... show me how you are using what you have been given to serve and honor God. Show me this, and I will show you a person who is truly rich!

These are the riches that matter.

These are the riches that moths and rust cannot destroy. They are everlasting!

I am not ashamed to say that absolutely everything of great magnitude I have ever accomplished in my adult life, was hiding in the secret place! It was in the secret place that God spoke to me and told me what to do. Let us never forget, even Jesus, as a baby, had to be hidden in Egypt until King Herod died and the timing was right for Him to return to Israel (Matthew 2:13-21).

So I say this to you, don't fight against God when He has chosen to hide you. Continue to do what He last told you to do until He reveals His timing and His will for your life. When you are hidden, maximize that opportunity by learning from Jesus, who at the age of twelve, "increased in wisdom and stature, and in favour with God and man" (Luke 2:52 KJV). The Bible teaches us "And ye shall seek me, and find me, when ye shall search for me with all your heart" (Jeremiah 29:13 KJV).

I pray that one day soon, God begins to reveal Himself to you in ways you never imagined and it changes your life forever.

May you always find comfort in the secret place, and may you always hide in the presence of God!

Hidden

Reflection:

The last thing I want in life is to be revealed too soon. I want to be ready for what God has for me. And if that means I must wait while He hides me, then I have learned to thank Him while I wait for His timing.

There is nothing more disheartening than to get what you want too soon, then lose it because your character couldn't handle the demand at that level and your spiritual muscles were not developed to withstand the pressure that comes along with it.

Recommended Reading:
- *In the shelter of your presence you hide them from all human intrigues; you keep them safe in your dwelling from accusing tongues* (Psalm 31:20 NIV).
- *For in the time of trouble he shall hide me in his pavilion: in the secret of his tabernacle shall he hide me; he shall set me upon a rock* (Psalm 27:5 KJV).
- *You are a hiding place for me; you preserve me from trouble; you surround me with shouts of deliverance. Selah* (Psalm 32:7 ESV).
- *That their hearts may be encouraged, having been knit together in love, and that they would attain to all the wealth that comes from the full assurance of understanding, resulting in a true knowledge of God's mystery, that is, Christ Himself, in whom are hidden all the treasures of wisdom and knowledge* (Colossians 2:2-3 NASB).

necessary.

- *He will cover you with his feathers, and under his wings you will find refuge; His faithfulness will be your shield and rampart* (Psalm 91:4 NIV).
- *And thou say in thine heart, My power and the might of mine hand hath gotten me this wealth. But thou shalt remember the LORD thy God: for it is he that giveth thee power to get wealth, that he may establish his covenant which he sware unto thy fathers, as it is this day* (Deuteronomy 8:17-18 KJV).
- *For in the day of trouble he will keep me safe in his dwelling; he will hide me in the shelter of his sacred tent and set me high upon a rock* (Psalm 27:5 NIV).

Assignment:

1. Write down what each passage means to you.

2. Can you identify any areas where you believe God is hiding you? If so, be specific.

3. What do you think God is preparing you for? In other words, what are you learning during this season of being hidden that can prepare you for what's to come?

4. When you survey all that God has done for you, how are you currently using what God has given you, to bring glory to Him?

Chapter 11

Affirmation – The Secret Place

I have found the secret place where my circumstances
Do not determine my destiny
And my fears and past failures cannot enter.

A place where I am no longer chained by my past.
A place where my naysayers cannot enter.

In this secret place
I am reminded that I can achieve all things.
I am reminded that I am greater than who I see in the mirror.

In this secret place
I am filled with love, wisdom, and great power!

This is my secret place…
In the presence of God!

[Audio/Video version of this book is available at ZenjaGlass.com]

Chapter 11
The Secret Place

God has shown me His secret place. In this place, I am able to walk with authority and kingship as I stand with my Father. In this place, I am not weak. I am strong! In this place, I am not vulnerable to attacks from the enemy. In this place, my finances do not get to determine my destiny! In this place, altars sent against me are commanded to fall, and the earth must yield to what God has predestined for my life!

I wish I could point to this location and say, "There it is!", but it cannot be seen with physical eyes. It is a secret place that flows in the presence of God. It is a secret place that raises us to levels that will completely transform our mind and elevate our Spirit in the presence of the Lord. This is a timeless place where we can stand with God and be filled with His power and great revelation.

This place is real! And when we are in this secret place, there are no fears, no problems, and no circumstances that can hold us down. From this place, we speak with authority as co-heirs with Jesus Christ [Yeshua] (Romans 8:17), as children of God (Galatians 3:26), as ambassadors for Christ (2 Corinthians 5:20), and as priests and kings (Revelations 5:10). From this place, we speak as those with dominion, power and authority (Genesis 1:26), and as those who know the Holy Spirit lives within us (Romans 8:11). From this place, the earth must yield (Psalm 67:6) and produce in the physical what has been proclaimed in the Spirit!

necessary.

Nothing just happens.

There is a secret place in the Spirit that proclaims what is to happen in the physical.

This secret place is revealed throughout our Bible... if only we would pay attention.

If you read Job chapter 1, there was a meeting concerning what was to happen to Job. Who attended that meeting, and where was that secret place?

Why did Queen Esther ask Mordecai and her fellow people to fast before approaching the king at the risk of her own life (Esther 4:15-16)? More importantly, who were they petitioning and where was that secret place?

Why did King David inquire of the Lord BEFORE he physically went into the battle (1 Samuel 30:8), (2 Samuel 5:19)? Who was he speaking to? Where was that secret place?

Who spoke to the prophet Samuel in 1 Samuel 16:1 and told him that he would be anointing a new king? Who told Samuel where to go find the new king? Where was that secret place between Samuel and the Lord?

John the Baptist prepared the way for the coming of the Lord (John 1). Where was that secret place where this was revealed to John the Baptist?

Where was the secret place where the prophet Isaiah received revelation and foretold the exact details of the coming of the Messiah, nearly 700 years before Mary gave birth to Jesus (Isaiah 53)?

How was Gideon able to win a war with only a few hundred men after the Lord reduced the size of his army (Judges 6-7)?

The Secret Place

Where was that secret place where Gideon heard from the Lord? Where was that secret place when God's strategy was revealed so that they could win the war?

Where was the secret place in Daniel 10:4-14 when he saw a vision, after the messenger from God was held up for 21 days while fighting the adversary?

Where was the meeting in the Spirit during the transfiguration, when the appearance of Jesus became "bright as a flash of lightning. Two men, Moses and Elijah, appeared in glorious splendor, talking with Jesus. They spoke about his departure, which he was about to bring to fulfillment at Jerusalem" (Luke 9:28-36 NIV). Where was that secret place?

Where was it?

There are countless examples of this secret place in the Bible. A place our physical eyes cannot see. A place where the Spirit of God dwells and mysteries are revealed. A place where we can see ourselves through the eyes of God. A place where we receive our strength. A place where we speak with power. A place where the earthly realm must submit. And dare I say, a place where meetings are held in the Spirit on our behalf.

From this secret place, we stand with the Father [Yahweh], the Son [Yeshua], and the Holy Spirit [Ruach Ha Kodesh]. From this secret place, we stand in the meetings concerning our future and we proclaim the words of God over our lives by quoting His words, and telling the earth it must produce what God has said!

From this secret place, we speak with the power and authority our Father in heaven has given to us. From this secret place, the heads of dragons and serpents are cut off, the arrows from the enemy are returned to them, and spirits of demonic

necessary.

influence are put on notice with the words of the Lord. This is how we fight in the Spirit (Ephesians 6:12-18)... in the secret place.

This is why we must pray continually, praise and worship God in song, meditate on His words day and night, and walk in obedience to His commands. We must spend time in the secret place where our circumstances are called to submit to higher levels in the Spirit. There are no fears in this place, and all wisdom and treasures give birth from its dwellings. This is where we belong!

In this secret place, where love and the almighty power of God reigns, we sit in His presence as we seek His wisdom and worship Him. In this place, the Spirit of God is drawn to sincere worship and praise. From this place of praise and worship, we hear the Lord repeating the words, "Because he has loved Me, I will save him; I will set him securely on high, because he has known My name" (Psalm 91:14 NASB).

In this secret place, God gives us wisdom and shows us the way to go. In this secret place, our days are planned and God speaks over our lives. From this place, expectations are set, instructions are given, and we receive what God has for us in the Spirit, before it is sent in the physical.

There is a sound that is heard in the secret place that the earth must obey! It is the sound of prayer, praise, and worship of God. It is the sound of the word of the Lord! We must search for this secret place as for hidden treasure (Proverbs 2:4). For it is written: "You will seek me and find me when you seek me with all your heart" (Jeremiah 29:13 NIV).

I was completely unaware of this higher level in the spiritual realm. When I heard people talk about this many years ago, I dismissed them as either exaggerating, or I simply placed them in a category of super-spiritual religious people who had some kind of special access to God that I had no chance of ever receiving. Either way, it didn't mean much to me because all I knew to do was pray, try my best to treat people right, and keep it moving. I always thought you had to be an ordained minister, evangelist, prophetess, or someone with a powerful title to receive that kind of "special access" to God.

God loves us, and He desires to have a close relationship with His children. I won't pretend to act as if I can give you a special formula for you to access this realm of the Spirit. Perhaps that is a conversation you can have with your minister, or with someone you trust to help you understand this a bit more. I can say, with great humility and truthfulness, that this secret place in the presence of God exists!

By the grace of God, I do my very best to meditate on His words, pray continually, obey His commands, and lift Him in song and praise as often as I can. I plead with the Lord to lift me and take me higher in the Spirit, so that I may know who I am and hear what He has to say. I wish I could express in words the peace that comes over me when I am in His presence, but there are no words created to explain it.

When we pray to God [Hebrew: *Yahweh*] in the name of Jesus Christ [Hebrew: *Yeshua*] by the power of the Holy Spirit [Hebrew: *Rauch Ha Kodesh*], there is a sound that is heard in the Spirit that will not return void (Isaiah 55:11). It does not return void because we serve a God of integrity, and what He says must be accomplished. When we speak His words, the sound of our prayers and praises produces a change in the atmosphere that petitions the presence of God to respond... and our circumstances must submit to His will!

necessary.

This is why praise and worship to God is so essential in our lives. In the secret place, we create an intimate relationship with God, a relationship that draws us closer together. We capture His attention as we spend time with Him, lifting Him in praise. And as we worship Him, He looks at us, moves in closer, and sees that, whether we are experiencing our greatest sorrows, pains, and disappointments in life, or on the mountaintop and rejoicing because we are in our seasons of reaping, we still praise Him and remain committed to Him. When He hears our prayers, sees our obedience, and knows our praises are sincere, He holds to His integrity and He responds! And like the jealous God that He is (Exodus 34:14, Exodus 20:5), He covers us with love, wisdom, treasures, power, and protection... in the secret place.

As a practical example, I end my day with Bible study, prayer and worship, and I start my day very early in the morning with the same process, including a prayer walk to go ahead of my day in the Spirit. What do I mean by going ahead in the Spirit?

When I go ahead of my day in the Spirit, I simply go into prayer and praise before God, in the secret place, and I discuss my day with the Lord so that the earth knows what to yield. It sounds a little weird to say it like that, but it's true. I have a right, as a son [daughter] of God, to attend the meetings concerning my day and lay my petition before the Lord. Seeking His wisdom is of utmost importance to me before I start my day. For those of you who might think that is a little too much to be doing, let me assure you of this, one word from the Lord is far more valuable to me than thousands of pieces of silver and gold.

I have heard the sound of His voice. I have felt the stare of His eyes. And though I mess up every single day in some way or the other, I seek His presence in the secret place and ask Him to order my steps because I know His words will never return void in my life. Every major thing I have ever accomplished was first spoken to me in the secret place.

I may not be able to convince you that this secret place is real. And you may be tempted to feel that I am just some religious woman hyping up a God that doesn't even exist. Or perhaps you may be tempted to feel, "Well, that's good for you. I haven't experienced that. I guess I am not righteous enough or religious enough." Please let me encourage you with this: I fall short every single day (Romans 3:23). I do not hold a religious title, nor a ministry license. I get tired. I get discouraged at times. I go through pruning seasons. And yes, I have felt I wasn't worthy of being in His presence as well, but God has shown me through countless examples in the Bible, that He specializes in using messed-up people (like me) for His good will.

I remember when God took me down a beautiful path of intense Bible study and He revealed to me some of the messed-up things His people did, but He loved them and still used them for His good will.

For example, Moses killed a man before being called to lead God's people out of Egypt (Exodus 2:11-12). King David slept with a married woman, got her pregnant, and intentionally had her husband, Uriah, killed by placing him on the front line during a war so that he could marry Bathsheba (2 Samuel 11). Abraham told Sarah (Sarai, his wife) on at least two occasions to say she was his sister because he feared he would be killed by other men because she was so beautiful (Genesis 12 and Genesis 20). The apostle Paul previously "persecuted the church of God and tried to destroy it" (Galatians 1:13 NIV).

necessary.

I could list more of these examples, but I hope you get the point. We are all messed up in some way or another, and many people we look up to in the Bible have also done a lot of wrong things, but that did not prevent them from being used by God.

I am grateful we serve a God who sees who we will become. This is why I love when the angel of the Lord called Gideon a mighty warrior (Judges 6:12) BEFORE he won the battle, when he saw himself as the weakest (Judges 6:15). This is why I also love what Jesus taught about "The Parable of the Lost Son" (Luke 15:11-32). The son requested his inheritance from his father. Then, he left his family and squandered his wealth in wild living. He messed up really badly and ended up with absolutely nothing. When the son finally came to his senses (vs. 17) and returned to his father, his father was filled with compassion. While his son was still a long way off, his father ran to him, welcomed him with open arms, put his best robe on him, and celebrated his return!

This is the love God has for us! Don't ever allow anyone to convince you that you have messed up too much to seek His presence. God loves you!

I urge you to seek His secret place while it may be found.

Reflection:

What if I were to tell you that there is a place where millions of dollars are stored and the secret to enjoyment of life dwelled, and it was buried in a treasure box in your backyard? How much time would you spend searching or digging for that secret place? I want to plead with you to search for this secret place in the Spirit as though for hidden treasures because once you discover this place, in the presence of God, where wisdom dwells, it will change your life forever!

This chapter is monumental for me because I did not know this secret place was real. I thought it was just something people made up to appear more religious than others, or perhaps it was reserved for people who were squeaky clean and never did anything wrong.

I pray you have been greatly encouraged to go deeper in your relationship with God... deeper into the secret place, where our Father stands and welcomes you with open arms.

Recommended Reading:

- *He that dwelleth in the secret place of the most High shall abide under the shadow of the Almighty* (Psalm 91:1 KJV).
- *For in the day of trouble he will keep me safe in his dwelling; he will hide me in the shelter of his sacred tent and set me high upon a rock* (Psalm 27:5 NIV).
- *But when you pray, go into your room, close the door and pray to your Father, who is unseen. Then your Father, who sees what is done in secret, will reward you* (Matthew 6:6 NIV).

necessary.

Assignment:

1. Take some time to reflect on this entire chapter and decide if you are willing to go deeper in your relationship with God and seek His secret place. What changes are you going to make in your life as a result of this decision?

2. If you have already discovered this secret place, what has God revealed to you? How has it changed your life?

Chapter 12

Affirmation – Caged Mindset

I've outgrown this cage.

It can no longer contain the greatness
God has inside of me.
I must fly higher to see
What's beyond my reflection in this mirror.

I must rise above what I thought was possible for my life.
I can't keep this limited mindset.

I am uncomfortable!
My dreams are too big for this tiny confinement!

It's time for me to fly!
God is calling me higher.

I've outgrown this cage!

[Audio/Video version of this book is available at ZenjaGlass.com]

Chapter 12

Caged Mindset

I recall visiting a traveling petting zoo a few years ago. It took me only a few minutes to notice almost all the cages were open. In some areas that housed roosters, chickens, rabbits, and so on, the top barriers were never even installed!

I asked the zookeeper how she keeps the chickens, rabbits and all the other animals from flying away or hopping out of their cages?

Her response startled me. She confidently said they won't leave their cages because they are conditioned to being in confined areas. She continued by saying that even when the doors are wide open and the barriers are completely removed, they won't fly away or attempt to leave because they have become accustomed to their cages.

I immediately felt compassion for the animals. I looked into their eyes and when the zookeeper wasn't paying any attention to me, I did my best to motion in such a way to show them the door was open. Everything in me wanted them to escape. A vast world was all around them, and open doors were only a few feet away, but they had been held in captivity for so long that none attempted to leave their cages. Even when they had several opportunities to explore the world beyond their barriers, they remained.

In fact, the zookeeper was so confident the animals wouldn't flee, she paid little attention to them as she greeted visitors, even though the cages were directly in front of open doorways. I forced myself to refrain from shouting at the animals to run. I saw

necessary.

escape routes everywhere! There was no way anyone could quickly catch them if they would just fly away. At the risk of looking foolish, I whispered to them, "You can get out of here if you want to." I whispered again, "Look up! Fly away! Hop out the door!"

I know they heard me... but they did not listen.

They did not understand.

They did not respond.

And as silly as this may sound, I would have helped protect them by distracting the zookeeper, had they only made an attempt to escape.

Instead, they remained caged. It was all they knew. They had no idea they could be free.

It is possible I wrongly assessed the situation, but to me, the animals seemed so unhappy. It was as if they were hopeless to even attempt to leave their current circumstances because they were conditioned to remain in those tight little spaces, surrounded by bars and fences, with little to no freedom to move about.

I am not implying the zookeeper was negligent in any way. Perhaps she took great care of the animals and kept them well fed. Some might even argue that perhaps she kept them safe and alive, away from predators or those who would harm them. It could all be true.

But there was something inside of me that felt great discomfort as I left the traveling farm that day. I almost wanted to cry because I remembered there was a time in my life when I had a caged mindset. I felt trapped, confined, with limited choices, and with very little willpower to do anything about it. Perhaps that's why I took it so personally because it reminded me of a time in life when I wasn't even aware that God had provided ways for me to not only stand, but to thrive when I felt I had no options available to me.

As I look back over my life, there were times when I never knew the door was open, the top barrier was missing, and my wings were strong enough to fly because I felt too powerless to look up. I was too frightened to step out on faith and see possibilities beyond my caged thinking, beyond what others may say about me if I dared to step outside the box built for me. The doors were always opened, but somehow, in the midst of all the worries and issues I was dealing with, I simply could not think beyond my circumstances because I was consumed with the woes of life. I was caged... and didn't even know it!

Do you have a caged mindset? Can you see beyond your current circumstances and free yourself to start imagining what looks like impossibilities to others?

Who told you that you were not capable of accomplishing something great? Who told you that you were thinking too big? Who told you that you have to stay on the career path your degree is in? Who told you that you have excelled far enough, and you shouldn't go any higher? Who told you that? Who put you in that cage?

I sincerely believe there are times when we limit the power of God at work in our lives because we are thinking too small. If you study any of the books of the Bible, you cannot deny the fact that God thinks generationally! He plans far beyond what is in front of us. This is why we must always humble ourselves before Him and sit in His presence for divine guidance. He sees what we cannot see, and He knows the path we should take. We must learn to not be afraid of thinking far beyond our current capabilities and start dreaming on levels that will impact generations to come. As

necessary.

many ministers have often stated, we must give God something to bless!

How can we adopt a higher mindset when everything we know is confined to our cages? Have you any idea how strange it was to believe a huge man-made machine could actually lift off the ground and fly in the air? Have you any idea of the complexities faced to invent the first three-position, T-shaped traffic signal? Have you any idea how silly it first sounded when people talked about sending a man to the moon? I can give countless examples of people, inventions, businesses, personal stories, and dreams that were accomplished because someone refused to remain in a caged, limited, status quo mindset. And despite what others said, they leaped and failed, and leaped and failed, time and time again, until they achieved desired results.

I challenge you to dream so high and reach so high, beyond your generation, beyond your caged thinking, that it captures the attention of God! We must get out of our cages and give Him something to work with! Let us never forget: "For as he thinketh in his heart, so is he" (Proverbs 23:7 KJV).

I speak passionately about this topic because, as a child, I experienced homelessness, witnessed countless abuses, and grew up in neighborhoods where most people wouldn't dare attempt to even walk down the street. But despite my upbringing, God had a plan for me. It took me years to break out of a caged mindset and go after dreams and goals that most people felt I could never achieve. God is able to do the impossible in our lives, but we must be willing to let go of the limitations we place on ourselves.

To this day, I still ask God to remove residues of caged thinking from my mind. I ask Him to bless me to think generationally... beyond my family... beyond my country... to think on levels that will impact people all over the world, for generations to come.

Caged Mindset

I ask Him to use me in ways that show the nations who He is. I ask Him to produce in me what will bless many others for years to come, not only spiritually, but mentally, economically, physically, and more. I want my multi-greats grandchildren to one day read my books or watch my videos and be pulled from dark places when they are challenged by the woes of life.

We must start thinking beyond our current circumstances. Beyond our cages. Beyond what others may view as impossible. We must reach so far into future generations that we capture God's attention!

It is my prayer that God opens your eyes as you examine your surroundings and use discernment so that you can know when and how to maximize your seasons. Ask yourself, have you outgrown your cage? Are you ready to soar to levels you've never seen? Do you believe the wisdom and favor of God over your life can take you higher?

We must never forget that James 4:14 (NIV) teaches us, "What is your life? You are a mist that appears for a little while and then vanishes." Therefore, it is my prayer that while there is still blood in our veins, we seek to deepen our relationship with God and start taking bold steps of faith as we soar beyond our caged thinking. We can't continue to fear what lies beyond the comfort of our cages. I am naïve enough to actually believe we can impact the entire world with the help of God! Are you?

No more caged thinking, my sisters and brothers. We have allowed limitations long enough in our lives. It is with sincere love and humility that I say to you, live before you die! Dream beyond what others define as possibilities in your life. Give God something to bless in this generation, and for generations to come!

necessary.

Reflection:

I am grateful God has opened my eyes to see beyond my confinements and to develop the courage to fly outside the cage I'd grown accustomed to. I will never forget the day I visited that petting zoo because it will always serve as my reminder to never allow anyone, nor any circumstance, to lock me in a cage and limit the power of God over my life. I will continue to become uncomfortable as I soar to new levels, until God decides to call me home!

Recommended Reading:

- *Whatever your hand finds to do, do it with all your might, for in the realm of the dead, where you are going, there is neither working nor planning nor knowledge nor wisdom* (Ecclesiastes 9:10 NIV).

- *But those who hope in the Lord will renew their strength. They will soar on wings like eagles; they will run and not grow weary, they will walk and not be faint* (Isaiah 40:31 NIV).

- *For nothing will be impossible with God* (Luke 1:37 ESV).

Assignment:

I'd like to do something a little different this time. I want you to spend some time reflecting over your life, and write a letter to yourself as if it were 20 years from now. Give yourself the advice

Caged Mindset

you believe you would give yourself 20 years from now. Then, read this letter aloud to yourself. The goal of this is to see if there are areas in your life where you can identify a caged mindset. After you have completed this, answer the questions below:

1. Did you discover any areas of your life where you had a caged mindset?

2. If so, what are those areas and how are you going to move forward?

[Audio/Video version of this book is available at ZenjaGlass.com]

Chapter 13

Affirmation – Letting Go

It's time for me to let go so that I can begin to live.

It's time for me to thrive in life

And receive all that God has in store for me.

I must let go of what no longer serves my destiny.

I must let go of my fears.

I must let go of my doubts.

I must lay all my burdens on the altar where they belong

In the hands of my Father who is meant to carry them.

I must let go.

I am a new creation.

And I must learn... to live!

[Audio/Video version of this book is available at ZenjaGlass.com]

Chapter 13

Letting Go

Sometimes, it feels so unnatural to start letting go.

Letting go of what I had in mind. Letting go of the outcomes I expected from all the love and hard work I poured into a person or a situation. Letting go of my version of myself and embracing what God desires for my life. Letting go of activities that do not serve my destiny. And letting go of those I love, whom God has called home. Sometimes it really hurts to let go, but if we live long enough, it is a process we all will experience at some point in our lives.

Letting go of what I had in mind is perhaps one of my greatest challenges. Life doesn't always turn out the way we predicted because the pathways to our destiny are seldom straight lines. It is so difficult to move out of the way and let God do what He does best… and that is, be God! We have to let God be God, not only when it comes to our lives, but also in the lives of others. We must remind ourselves that it is not our responsibility to play His role in the lives of our loved ones. And I know firsthand, this can be very difficult when it comes to our closest relationships.

It took me nearly 50 years to understand that letting go is an act of love, not only for others, but for ourselves as well. Sometimes, we may not realize how much stress and anxiety can impact us mentally, physically, and spiritually until we begin to show symptoms. It wasn't until I began to let go of situations in my life, and place a greater priority on my well-being and in my walk with God, that I saw the magnitude of the pressures I was trying to carry. This is why we have to pray for God to open our eyes

necessary.

because sometimes the enemy wants us to feel like superheroes, and trick us into believing it is our role to be "God" for other people.

When I love someone, I love hard. It doesn't matter if they are family members, friends, or strangers. I naturally take care of people and want their needs to be met. And when I care for someone, I am willing to do almost anything to help them. After all, God calls us to love one another (John 15:12-13) and I wholeheartedly believe we are to serve and help each other, even during difficult times. I guess that's why it hurts so badly when the time comes to let go... even when I know it is the will of God.

I recall numerous times throughout my life when I tried to keep others from making mistakes and facing dire consequences that, in my opinion, could have been avoided. But sometimes, as difficult as it is to admit this, when we think we are helping others, we could be preventing them from experiencing what they need to experience so that they can grow and learn from their mistakes. I know that's difficult for many of us to accept because, as we all know, some mistakes are irreversible. And at times, it is frightening to trust that God will take care of them, especially when they make decisions that can have a tremendous impact on their lives. However, when all is said and done, the fact remains, we can't make anyone do anything they are not willing to do.

This is why we must have healthy boundaries. There are times when we must distance ourselves from unhealthy patterns and toxic relationships that wreak havoc in our lives. Sometimes, even our loved ones can drain us with their issues. And if we continue to allow chaos and confusion in our lives, with no healthy boundaries in place, we can easily find ourselves becoming overwhelmed. We can become so distracted that we can't even hear what God is trying to tell us, nor see the hand of the enemy at work to keep us from walking in our purpose.

It took me many years to realize this because for most of my life I walked around with my spiritual eyes closed. I was unaware, or should I say, I forgot, that spiritual forces of evil in the heavenly realms were always at work (Ephesians 6:12). The Bible teaches us that we must watch our lives and doctrines closely (1 Timothy 4:16) and we must be aware that Satan masquerades as an angel of light (2 Corinthians 11:14). He will attempt to use anyone, or any situation to keep us from staying in the race and being self-disciplined (1 Corinthians 9:24-27).

One of my favorite Bible verses states:

"Therefore, since we are surrounded by such a great cloud of witnesses, let us throw off everything that hinders and the sin that so easily entangles, and let us run with perseverance the race marked out for us" (Hebrews 12:1-2 NIV).

I don't have a problem with letting go and turning things over to God by placing my burdens on His altar and walking away. I have a problem with going back to that altar and picking them up again when I think I need to take them back because God isn't fixing them the way I think they should be fixed, or He isn't moving fast enough for me. It sounds really bad to say this, but in essence, that's what it looks like to me when I start worrying and allowing myself to become stressed over situations I can't control.

Have you ever felt that you are the only person who can take care of a situation? And instead of getting help or training others, you wear yourself out all day long trying to remain in control of everything. If you can relate to this, I strongly recommend that you learn from our brother Moses. Exodus 18 is an important chapter in the Bible because it tells the story of Jethro, the priest and father-in-law of Moses, who visited him and realized Moses was taking on far more than he could handle. Whenever the

necessary.

people had disputes, Moses served as their only judge from morning till evening. Though Moses was trying to help them, he was unaware that in the process of trying to serve so many people, he was wearing himself out. Moses' father-in-law had to help him to realize that he needed to appoint capable men to serve as judges over the smaller cases so that he would have a lighter load.

Isn't it interesting that someone had to bring this to Moses' attention? Sometimes we can become so consumed with putting out fires and fixing problems, that we don't even realize we are wearing ourselves out, and we need to lighten our loads so that we can have enjoyment in life.

If we can just remember to lay our burdens on the altar and leave them there, we could save ourselves a tremendous amount of pain and grief. I know that's easier said than done. However, there is a reason God teaches us to "Cast all your anxiety on Him, because He cares about you" (1 Peter 5:7 NASB). The burden belongs with God. He is capable of holding what we were not meant to carry. He invites us to put the weight of our worries on His shoulders so that we can be free to rise.

I had to come to the realization that letting go of relationships doesn't mean you no longer care, love, or pray for others. In fact, I have prayed more for some people after they have been set free from my life than when they were in my presence. Why? Because God is able to give us a heart of compassion to pray for those who have hurt us... even when they won't admit to causing any harm. And just to be clear, I am not in any way advocating to become best friends or welcome those people in your home again. I am simply saying that it is possible to let people go without hating them so that you can be free to rise to higher levels.

So, what do we do when we have done all we can?

Before you think about that question, let me make this statement: The Bible teaches us to stand (Ephesians 6:13) and always pray (Ephesians 6:18). I strongly believe in the power of prayer, and I believe that we should continuously pray, on all occasions, as God calls us to do in 1 Thessalonians 5:17. Prayer is powerful! I also believe we are able to intercede for others, and if it is the will of God, we are able to move His heart to respond to our faithful prayers.

Now let me be a little bit more specific with my question: What do you do when your life has become consumed with trying to change a person or a situation, and you have worn yourself out because you are carrying their loads?

I had to learn the hard way to stop playing the role of God, and let go. God had to teach me how to let go of situations that didn't have my name on it. And just to be clear, that does not mean I stopped praying for them. But I have learned that I don't have a right to deny others the opportunity to grow.

I remember a time in my life when I allowed everyone's problem to become my problem because I didn't want anyone to be inconvenienced. For example, if someone I loved was completely undisciplined with their finances, I would deny myself and give them money so that they could purchase what they needed or pay a bill. In the name of love, I wouldn't let them suffer any consequences because I felt guilty if I was able to help them and didn't bail them out. I felt it was the Christian thing to do because we are to help one another... right?

The problem was, the cycle continued because they would consistently spend outside their means and then run to me again and again to solve their urgent financial needs, because they knew I wouldn't say no. It took me years to finally realize that their emergencies did not need to become my emergencies, and the help I thought I was giving them was actually enabling them

necessary.

to continue the pattern. I ended up becoming so exhausted. Somehow, I felt it was my role to be their hero. I got to a point where I couldn't even stay focused on what God had planned for me to do because I was too busy playing God in their lives!

I was so wrapped up in their mess by trying to keep them on the right track, that I didn't even realize my own finances were suffering, my prayer life was suffering, and I was taking on loads I wasn't meant to carry. I wasn't reading my Bible as often as I used to, I was always in a state of anxiousness and nervousness, and I certainly was not at peace in my spirit so that I could receive the direction God had for my life. Can anyone relate to this?

Can anyone relate to being so consumed in the lives of others, that you barely have a life of your own? This is common for those of us who love hard. We sincerely care for the well-being of others, and without realizing it, we find ourselves sitting on the throne in their lives because we moved God out of their way and taught them to run to us to fix all their problems. And we wonder why we feel so tired and exhausted most of the time. We are carrying loads we were never meant to carry!

There was a time in my life when I was consumed with keeping some of my loved ones from getting into heated arguments with each other, and it began to wear me down. I can't count the number of days I thought to myself: If they would just listen to me, they could avoid a bad situation from happening.

I will never forget the day I talked with my sister about this. She is an amazing woman of God. She said to me, "Z, you are the target... not them!" That stung so badly, but I needed to hear it. I needed to feel it because it shocked me and woke me up. It opened my eyes to the true spiritual battle that was taking place. I was consumed with trying to prevent what could happen to those I loved. I was so wrapped up in trying to keep arguments down, and keep them from making mistakes that could have

Letting Go

ended them in trouble, that I was losing sight of my own life. In my attempt to run their lives, I forgot I had one of my own! I wasn't paying attention to what God was trying to manifest in my own life.

The real target was me! The enemy was trying to keep me distracted so that my eyes would not be on the Lord.

But how do you let go of someone you love without feeling guilty? And is that even possible?

In all sincerity and honesty, I haven't quite figured it all out, but I have certainly gained a healthy, spiritual perspective about how God calls me to respond. This valuable lesson can be found in Galatians 6:2-5. It clearly teaches us the difference between burdens and loads, and it helps us to make wise decisions about what we are meant to carry, and what is meant for others to carry for themselves.

Galatians 6:2-5 (ESV) starts off by teaching us that we are to carry each other's *burdens*, but it ends by stating each person should bear their own *load*. For a deeper understanding, you can research the Greek translation of those words for yourself; however, I will do my best to explain it as I understood it from my Bible lessons years ago.

I never knew there was a difference between a burden and a load because I always thought it would be selfish of us who claim to be Christians and not meet every need that arises around us. If you study this, you will discover in the King James version, the word "burden" is used twice in the same passage; however, the words have different meanings. Burdens are situations that can be very oppressive to carry alone, such as a recent medical diagnosis, and relying on others to help you with the care that you need. As believers in the word of God, we are to carry each other's burdens and take care of each other.

necessary.

Loads are often seen as issues that people must take personal responsibility for. An example of this can be someone consistently overspending and being completely undisciplined with their finances, but always asking for money because they know they can get it from you by making you feel guilty if you don't help them. At some point, that person must take responsibility and carry his own load. That is not a burden others should continue to carry for them.

While there are certainly exceptions to all of this, these have become my general guidelines that God has taught me so that I can discern, "Is this something I should be carrying? Is this something I must now let go of?" I am naturally a giver, and I strive to meet needs when I can, but by the grace and wisdom of God, I have finally learned the value of the word *No* without strings of guilt being attached to it. I have finally realized that it is okay to put down loads I was not meant to keep carrying... and let God complete His work in the lives of others.

And let us not forget, we also have to let go of the old version of ourselves so that we can rise and live a life that brings glory and honor to God. That includes letting go of spiritual strongholds, counterfeit gods, idols, and harmful activities that no longer serve our destiny. The Bible teaches us, "If anyone is in Christ, the new creation has come: The old has gone, the new is here" (2 Corinthians 5:17 NIV).

I know firsthand how appeasing those counterfeit gods can be. They feel so good. They bring such pleasure. And they hide so well! They try to convince us that we are not strong enough to let them go, and that we need them. They try to coerce us into believing that God isn't powerful enough to free us from their grip. But we must let them go. We must let go so that we can honor God and live a life that is pleasing to Him. Satan, the father of lies, desires to destroy us (Luke 22:31-32). He hides in the darkness, hoping that we will never... let him go.

Lastly, sometimes, people may let us go! If that ever happens, I encourage you to seek God for wisdom and insight, and find out if you did anything wrong. It doesn't matter if it was intentional or unintentional. It is so important to God that we respond in humility and seek forgiveness when we have wronged someone. And I know that's difficult to do, especially when you can easily point out the wrongs they did as well. But there is a passage in the Bible that always humbles me when I am tempted to focus on what someone else has done in order to justify my wrongdoings.

Jesus stated in Matthew 7:3-4 (NIV):

"Why do you look at the speck of sawdust in your brother's eye and pay no attention to the plank in your own eye? How can you say to your brother, 'Let me take the speck out of your eye,' when all the time there is a plank in your own eye?"

That is such a powerful statement from Jesus as He reminds us to be careful when we judge others instead of looking to ourselves first. This is why we should always walk in love and humility as we let go of others, and if the time should come, as they let go of us. Life has taught me that both scenarios can be a blessing. For this reason, when someone decides to walk out of my life, I have learned to open the door very wide, because some people are meant to be a part of our lives for only a season.

I pray that you have learned a thing or two from this chapter. I pray that, in the face of whatever may be keeping you up in the midnight hours, causing you to lose sleep, and prompting you to worry; you find comfort and peace in God as you let go and put it all in His hands. I know firsthand that sometimes life can throw us curve balls and we can find ourselves dealing with situations that we never thought we would ever experience.

necessary.

But I want to remind you again, life is short (James 4:14), we are just passing through. Jesus came so that we can have life, and have it to the fullest (John 10:10).

There is a secret prayer that I say to God at certain times in my life. It is about letting go of all that I cannot control so that I can actually enjoy my life during my time on this earth. It is a very short prayer that encourages my spirit. While it may seem odd to pray such a prayer, it actually gives me peace, and it reminds me to appreciate the precious time we have all been given.

My short prayer is: "Dear God, please teach me how to live before I die."

Reflection:

Letting go means that I must trust God is greater than I am, and I must trust that His supreme wisdom and will for my life and my loved ones is at work... even when it doesn't feel like it.

As I reflect on all those years of worrying and stressing over people and situations, I now realize, God's plan still prevailed. And while I certainly do not regret loving others and pouring my time, resources, and efforts into helping people, I am now learning the art of letting go, and the fallacy of trying to hold on to what I cannot and should not attempt to control.

Finally, I am learning to let go.

Finally, I am learning to live!

Letting Go

Recommended Reading:

- *There is a time for everything, and a season for every activity under the heavens* (Ecclesiastes 3:1 NIV).
- *Bear one another's burdens, and so fulfill the law of Christ. For if anyone thinks he is something, when he is nothing, he deceives himself. But let each one test his own work, and then his reason to boast will be in himself alone and not in his neighbor. For each will have to bear his own load* (Galatians 6:2-5 ESV).
- *For the moment, all discipline seems not to be pleasant, but painful; yet to those who have been trained by it, afterward it yields the peaceful fruit of righteousness* (Hebrews 12:11 NASB).
- *But each person is tempted when he is lured and enticed by his own desire. Then desire when it has conceived gives birth to sin, and sin when it is fully grown brings forth death* (James 1:14-15 ESV).
- *No man can serve two masters: for either he will hate the one, and love the other; or else he will hold to the one, and despise the other. Ye cannot serve God and mammon* (Matthew 6:24 KJV).

Assignment:

1. Can you identify any areas of your life where you need to let go and trust God in the situation? If so, what are they?

2. How do you plan on establishing healthy boundaries in your life?

3. Can you identify any loads that do not belong to you? If so, please list them. Are you willing to seek advice, pray to God, and ask for wisdom to put them down?

[Audio/Video version of this book is available at ZenjaGlass.com]

Chapter 14

Affirmation – I Won't Apologize for Going Higher!

I won't apologize for going higher!
I won't apologize for dreaming so big
That it makes others uncomfortable.

I won't apologize for reaching so high
That I must elevate and be completely transformed!

I can't apologize for going HIGHER
Because my Father has created me to soar!

Therefore... I must rise!

[Audio/Video version of this book is available at ZenjaGlass.com]

Chapter 14

I Won't Apologize for Going Higher!

There was a time in my life when I allowed fears to keep me from dreaming beyond my circumstances because I didn't want to offend those who felt they knew where I belonged. Somehow, I felt guilty for wanting to go higher. I didn't want anyone to feel uncomfortable by seeing me rise to higher levels because I feared it would not only challenge the way they viewed me, but also the way they viewed themselves. So, I apologized for going higher... by staying low.

I wasn't willing to admit it at the time, but somehow I had a fear of actually succeeding and that scared me, because I knew that not everyone in my surroundings would be able to accept, appreciate, or love me at a higher level. I didn't want to leave anyone behind. I didn't want anyone to be jealous or envious of me, and I certainly didn't want anyone to be offended by my audacity to dream beyond their version of me. So, I stayed low... a little longer.

As I walked closer with God and placed my security in Him, I realized I didn't owe anyone an apology for elevating and becoming a better version of myself. It was not my responsibility to maintain how others perceived me, nor force them to accept who I was becoming. It is my responsibility to humbly walk in step with the Holy Spirit and to unapologetically live a life pleasing to God by serving Him with my gifts and talents as I walk in the direction that He leads me. I won't apologize for that. And I can't apologize to those who struggle with my refusal to remain

necessary.

stagnant. I can't apologize because God has predestined me to fulfill His purpose, and I must rise to His call!

As I began to focus on how I could use my gifts and talents to serve God, I had to allow God to transform me, even when it upset others. One of the biggest hurdles I had to overcome was letting go by allowing people to think whatever they chose to think about me as I began to set healthy boundaries in my life. I had to let go of responding to accusations about my character. I had to let go of desires and activities that held me down. I had to let go of the fear of disappointing those I loved by not remaining in the boxes they built for me. I had to let go of past failures and try again.

And most importantly, I had to let go of me. I had to die to my pride, arrogance, and what I thought was best for my life by placing God in the driver's seat and trusting His navigation. There is a time in life when we must spiritually mature from milk to solid foods (1 Corinthians 3:2). Simply going to church and praying a few times a week did not satisfy my desire to walk closer with the Lord. I needed more... more of Him and less of me (John 3:30).

I had to go higher. Higher in my prayer life and higher in my worship and praise to Him. That was not easy to do because I experienced many hardships and setbacks, and the thought of trusting God's "master plan" for my life, without me approving the blueprint, was a scary concept.

But I couldn't stay low. I couldn't continue to simply wonder what my life would be like if I truly threw off everything that hindered me and aimed for higher grounds. A higher prayer life. A higher mindset. A higher version of myself that completely transformed my life.

I just couldn't stay low any longer by walking safely along the sidelines, never really going all in to pursue my dreams, and aiming to please others instead of pleasing God and His purpose for my life. A Bible passage that really changed my outlook on life was Ecclesiastes 9:10, believed to have been written by King Solomon. It states: "Whatever your hand finds to do, do it with all your might, for in the realm of the dead, where you are going, there is neither working nor planning nor knowledge nor wisdom." In an earlier chapter, he also wrote "For death is the destiny of everyone; the living should take this to heart" Ecclesiastes 7:2 (NIV).

That passage rocked me to my core because it helped me to realize we are all here for only a moment (James 4:14). The only time we have to do any work under the sun is the time between the day we are born and the day we take our last breath. And I was determined to make the best of every day given to me.

The more I realized how short and precious life is, the more I developed the courage to unapologetically strive to live life to the fullest by honoring God and using His precious talents to achieve dreams beyond my imagination. Perhaps this is why I love the "Parable of the Talents." It is an amazing parable in Matthew 25 that reminds us to use what God has freely given us, for His good will.

In that parable, Jesus told the story of a man entrusting his property to his servants. He gave the first person five talents, the second two talents, and the third received one talent. He expected them to invest what he gave them. When the man returned, he was pleased with the first two servants because they doubled his investment. However, the servant who was given one talent did not produce a return on investment. In fear, he buried the talent in the ground, and when the man returned, he gave it back to him. That servant who was given the one talent received a major rebuke for being fearful and refusing to invest the talent that was given to him (Matthew 25). I like reflecting on this parable when I am tempted to give in to fear because it contains so many hidden gems that we can apply to our everyday

necessary.

lives. It reminds me to use my God-given gifts to advance His kingdom and His purpose for my life.

I had to take a chance and see what could become of my life if I leaned in to trust Him more... if I stopped looking back at what didn't work and focused on what was possible. I was determined to soar because destiny refused to be caged any longer. The more I began to take steps of faith and use my God-given talents, the more God showed me that when I put Him first in my life and commit all my plans to Him, what others saw as impossible would be mine.

I had to make changes in my daily routine by refusing to participate in negative, fruitless conversations that lacked elevation. I refused to engage in random arguments and battles that had no trophy. Every time I looked up, Destiny was standing at my door, motioning for me to move forth, calling me higher! No one else in my surroundings seemed to notice her standing there, but I was well aware of her presence, and I responded to her call.

Not everyone in my life was pleased with this newfound path I was on. But I could not apologize for refusing to surrender to their old version of me. I so badly wanted to say: "Don't you see that I've changed? Don't you see how God has changed me to be His reflection? So how can I possibly walk like I used to walk? How can I talk like I used to talk? And how can I do what I used to do, when He has changed me?" This is why I couldn't apologize for going higher. No apologies were necessary because God was taking me to higher grounds.

Each time God called me a little higher, I noticed He detached someone or something from me, even if it only involved detaching me from myself... from my flawed patterns of behaviors and beliefs that held me back. But I had to go higher, and I won't apologize for that. In fact, why should we ever apologize for imitating our Father in heaven?

As I began to focus on honoring God in my life, I had to close doors that led me down dark pathways. I had to allow some unhealthy relationships to end. And at times, I had to disappoint others by not always being available to return a call, reply to a message, attend events, or respond to any drama that didn't impact my destiny!

I had to change my schedule, adjust my routines, and set limitations on what was worthy of my attention because I needed to get quiet and hide with my Father so that I could hear what He was saying. I had to hear what He was saying because I was tired of wandering around in the desert, in a dry land filled with false promises, setbacks, and heartaches.

I am sorry that I cannot be sorry.

I won't ever apologize for going higher!

Reflection:

I had to remember that God gave a dream to me, and it was not my responsibility to make anyone believe it or support it. It was my responsibility to walk in faith, humility, love, and obedience to God by using the talents He gave me to serve Him and help others come to know Him.

As I spent more time in prayer, studying my Bible, and sitting silently in the presence of God, He began to whisper words of wisdom to me. I did not have a clear roadmap, nor the resources to make some bold moves God placed in my heart to do, but I

necessary.

refused to allow my circumstances, and yes, even naysayers, to stop me from going higher.

I stand and declare, as we seek to walk in alignment with the purpose God has for our lives, He not only orders our steps, but He also provides the provisions along the way. He desires to bless our lives in ways we can only imagine.

If only we would stop apologizing for going higher.

If only we would be willing… to rise!

Recommending Reading:

- *You are a mist that appears for a little while and then vanishes* (James 4:14 NIV).
- *For he chose us in him before the creation of the world to be holy and blameless in his sight. In love he predestined us for adoption to sonship through Jesus Christ* (Ephesians 1:4-5 NIV).
- *For those God foreknew he also predestined to be conformed to the image of his Son* (Romans 8:29 NIV).
- *Therefore, since we are surrounded by such a great cloud of witnesses, let us throw off everything that hinders and the sin that so easily entangles. And let us run with perseverance the race marked out for us, fixing our eyes on Jesus, the pioneer and perfecter of our faith* (Hebrews 12:1-2 NIV).
- *But one thing I do: Forgetting what is behind and straining toward what is ahead, I press on toward the goal to win the prize for which God has called me heavenward in Christ Jesus* (Philippians 3:13-14 NIV).
- *He that walketh with wise men shall be wise* (Proverbs 13:20 KJV).

- Read the entire "Parable of the Talents" in Matthew 25:14-30.

Assignment:

1. Can you identify any areas in your life where you are not putting forth your best effort because you are concerned about the opinion of others? If so, be specific.

2. Can you identify any obstacles that block you from achieving higher goals or, perhaps, from achieving your dreams in life? If so, be specific.

3. Can you identify any obstacles that prevent you from growing in your relationship with God? If so, be specific.

4. What commitment are you willing to make today as a result of what you have just learned?

[Audio/Video version of this book is available at ZenjaGlass.com]

Chapter 15

Affirmation – The Price of Elevation

I can't stay in this familiar territory

Where stagnation has become the norm.

I must pay the price of elevation by allowing God to detach

What is no longer needed for my next level.

I can't stay in this familiar territory

I was created for so much more!

I was created for more than what my eyes currently see.

I was created to thrive and achieve what may seem impossible to others.

Do you hear that?

Do you hear that sound from above?

It is the sound of our victories

That have already been won!

It is the sound of ELEVATION!

[Audio/Video version of this book is available at ZenjaGlass.com]

Chapter 15

The Price of Elevation

Elevation comes with a price tag, and that price is called detachment. It is not an easy price to pay because we must detach from our will and become less, as God becomes more. When God is honored and exalted, He defends His integrity and magnifies Himself in every area of our lives by calling us higher. This is what it means to elevate! But the question we all must answer is: Are you willing to detach to go higher?

Sometimes that detachment is from people in our lives who were sent for only a season. Sometimes that detachment is from unhealthy behaviors or bad habits that grieve the Holy Spirit (Ephesians 4:30). And sometimes we have to detach from ourselves… our wants… our plans… and our desires (Luke 14:33).

Even though it hurts to detach, I've discovered it hurts even more to refuse to rise and, instead, to remain stagnant. It hurts so badly, especially when everything in us wants to stay comfortable… even if comfortable isn't really comfortable at all.

It's strange to admit this, but if we are truly honest with ourselves, sometimes we want to hold on to that behavior, that person, or that old mindset because it's familiar or, dare I say, safe? And it's during those moments of making those faithful, scary, and at times, nerve-wrecking decisions to let go, that we realize, it is not only necessary for our spiritual growth, but also necessary to keep us from remaining static with unfulfilled dreams and delayed destinies.

necessary.

Not everyone is willing to pay the price of elevation, and you have to be okay with that. It hurts to see a loved one refuse to detach from old ways, old habits, and in some cases, harmful behaviors that greatly impact not only themselves, but their families as well. But some people are happy just the way things are, and they are not willing to let go of what holds them down, to reach for higher levels.

So what do you do if God is calling you higher, but your loved ones don't hear the call nor take any interest in rising? What do you do if your community of friends and loved ones become resentful or criticize you as you aim for higher grounds? And how do you handle the pressures of being transformed, when those in your environment are complacent and begin to become uncomfortable with this newer version of you?

The answer is quite clear.

You must rise anyway!

You must pay the price of elevation... by detaching from spiritual strongholds... and rise!

As you start rising, some people may have a huge problem with that. They may withhold their love, take away their support, misunderstand your intentions, or try to talk you out of pursuing the dream God gave you because it doesn't line up with their version of who you can become.

Who are you to rise? Who do you think you are? Do you think you are better than us? Those are some of the thoughts their actions may show, but the question I ask you again is: Are you willing to pay the price? Can you detach from spiritual strongholds that are sent to keep you from rising, or will you stay low, and continue to appease the desires of others so no one will become uncomfortable in your presence?

The Price of Elevation

Now, before you start kicking people out of your house and changing your phone number, I don't think it is my place to tell you what to do in your relationships. I trust that you will seek the help from God and, if needed, from professionals to help you make the best decisions for your life.

Detaching does not always mean you have to walk away from people or remove them entirely from your life, but let's not confuse that with detaching from those who are on assignments as spiritual strongholds to keep us from lifting and glorifying God. Absolutely nothing shall be able to separate us from the love of God (Romans 8:38-39). This is why we must always pray (1 Thessalonians 5:17), seek advice (Proverbs 15:22), ask God for discernment (Psalm 119:66), and walk in love and humility (Ephesians 5:2) as we make the decisions to develop healthy boundaries or detach from harmful relationships in our lives.

Sometimes detaching meant I had to let go of people and never look back again, especially in unhealthy relationships with poor boundaries that others were not willing to respect. I did not know it was possible to detach from people and still love and pray for them. It was very painful during those seasons of my life because I just couldn't understand why some people were unwilling to love me enough to respect my boundaries. But when God calls us higher, we can't stay low to appease others. And we can't stay low to comfort ourselves. We must pay the price of elevation by trusting His plan for our lives, and rise... unapologetically!

While it hurts... still rise! While everything in you wants to fix them... still rise! While you look to yourself and feel the loneliness... still rise! While you cry... still rise! While you are not confident in yourself and unsure of where God is taking you... still rise! And while you are afraid because you don't know His full plan... still rise!

necessary.

We. Must. Rise.

We were never created to remain stagnant. We were never created to worry. We were created to worship God [Yahweh], our Father in Heaven, and walk in alignment with His will for our lives. I know at times, the scales may seem so imbalanced, especially for those on this journey with little to no support. And it can be even more difficult when you have a tremendous number of responsibilities and others are depending on you, but I want to encourage you with these two scriptures:

- *Let us not become weary in doing good, for at the proper time we will reap a harvest if we do not give up* (Galatians 6:9 NIV).
- *Therefore, since we are surrounded by such a great cloud of witnesses, let us throw off everything that hinders and the sin that so easily entangles. And let us run with perseverance the race marked out for us, fixing our eyes on Jesus, the pioneer and perfecter of faith* (Hebrews 12:1-2 NIV).

As we become less and God becomes more, we are challenged to detach from unhealthy behaviors and harmful activities that do not bring honor to God (Galatians 5:19-21). We have to be courageous enough to look in the mirror and ask ourselves if we are willing to pay that price? Ask yourself, are you really willing to pay the price of elevation by lifting the King of kings above yourself? Or will you continue to be your own king? (1 Timothy 6:15, Revelations 17:14).

Detaching from ourselves can be just as difficult as detaching from others. Why? Because it involves letting go of old mindsets, old patterns, and repenting of our sins as we walk in obedience and honor God in our lives. I won't attempt to tell you what that should look like for you, but I can certainly speak of my own experiences.

The Price of Elevation

For me, that price involved accepting Jesus Christ [Yeshua] as my Lord and Savior. That price involved spending quality time to go deeper in my relationship with Him instead of gambling in casinos or indulging in pleasures that left me feeling empty inside. That price involved learning how to forgive others and show compassion when everything in me wanted to seek revenge.

That price involved humbling myself before the Lord and surrendering at the foot of the cross, even when my world seemed so dark, when some of my loved ones passed away, when I felt so alone, when I felt so unloved, and when nothing made any sense to me at all... I laid it all down. I surrendered and put it all in His hands. It was, and is, a heavy price to pay, but I have discovered, when I cast all my burdens on Him, He seems more than willing to carry them for me (Matthew 11:28-30, 1 Peter 5:7, Psalm 55:22). And each time I lift Him higher, He takes me with Him... far above my pain... far above my circumstances... and far above what I thought could ever be possible for my life.

If you are interested in a few practical examples of paying the price of elevation, I will share some of the changes God led me to make in my life:

I sought to go higher in my understanding of not only who God is, but who I am in His presence. In my humble opinion, Jesus Christ [Yeshua] paid a heavy price for me to have that opportunity to know Him, and I had to pay the price by simply spending time with Him, so that I could be free to see myself through His eyes and finally starting dreaming again! I needed to know what He saw in me because there was a time in my life when I had no one to remind me of who I was, or who I could become.

Additionally, I changed the way I spent my downtime. Watching episodes of my favorite shows and spending hours on social media never left me feeling fulfilled in life.

necessary.

The bible teaches us "And ye shall seek me, and find me, when ye shall search for me with all your heart" (Jeremiah 29:13 KJV). So, I decided to put pressure on God's integrity to see if He would truly reveal Himself in my life. I spent countless hours in my closet pouring out my heart to Him, praying, reading my bible, meditating on His scriptures, confessing my sins, asking for wisdom, and begging Him to reveal Himself to me.

You would not be reading or listening to this book right now if that heavy price wasn't paid. Why? Because I would have nothing to say. I would have no fire or wisdom from God to pass on to you. I would have no victories to claim because I would still be steep in the worries of life, trying to fight my battles without the proper spiritual weapons (Ephesians 6:12).

I cannot end this chapter without addressing business owners, entrepreneurs, future leaders, and those who are in leadership positions around the world. We must be the ultimate example of treating people with love, dignity, and respect. Our lives must be living examples of what it looks like to be leaders who remain committed to God even after our needs have been met. While this may seem easy, I can assure you, for many people, it is a heavy price they are not willing to pay.

Will you still speak of His glory even when it is not common among your peers? Will you still remember to bring praise and honor to God, even when your barns are overflowing? Or is He only your God when you are in the valleys?

In my humble opinion, I believe God is willing to put in us whatever will flow through us. I sincerely believe, when God knows His investment in us will bring Him glory and honor, and He knows we won't covet or worship other gods before Him, there is nothing He won't do for us because He knows we will use whatever He gives us to honor Him, and bless others. May we never be afraid to proclaim all that God has done in our lives.

The Price of Elevation

As children of God [Yahweh] who are called to be leaders, we must pay the price of elevation by not only walking closely with Him, but also by devoting the time to gain wisdom. In my old, limited mindset, I placed limitations on what I could learn from others because I wasn't mature enough to realize that God could also work through others to teach me. I wasn't mature enough to realize that I also needed to gain wisdom by learning from those who have mastered what I was trying to accomplish.

As a practical example, I started watching educational videos, reading more books, and attending seminars, not only to grow in my relationship with God, but also to develop better leadership skills, implement proven business systems and processes to improve workflows, and seek financial advice, etc. I had to detach from fantasizing about a life I wanted and start walking in obedience to God by humbling myself to learn from others, including mentors, advisors, and business leaders who loved God and set amazing examples for me to follow.

That was, and is, a heavy price to pay for elevation because I had to swallow my pride and allow God to train me in the areas that were not my greatest strengths. He used other people to teach me new skills, better procedures, and proven processes so that I could be a good steward over managing my business and my resources for His glory, and to help others in need. I am so grateful that God humbled me to acknowledge my weaknesses and seek help so that I could finally detach from a very limited, scarcity mindset, and embrace possibilities that I could not see. The Bible teaches us, "As iron sharpens iron, so one person sharpens another" (Proverbs 27:17 NASB).

Lastly, I never knew that God cared so much about how we treat our bodies, the temple of the Holy Spirit (1 Corinthians 6:19-20). It is so important that we pay the price of elevation by also taking good care of ourselves by eating better foods, exercising, etc.

necessary.

While I certainly fall short in this area, and need to continue to improve, I know it is important that we take care of ourselves mentally, spiritually, and physically, so that we can be present in the new territories God has stored up for us.

So, what does all this have to do with elevation? Everything. Absolutely everything!

If we are to become thought leaders and people who can influence and impact nations, we must strive to excel in everything we do. In doing so, we can multiply what God has entrusted to us, as we continue to spread His word and help others all over the world. I say with strong conviction: "Unless the Lord builds the house, its builders labor in vain" Psalm 127:1 (NIV). Elevation means nothing if God is not elevating with us as our territories are enlarging and our barns are overflowing. We must never become a swampland by preventing blessings from flowing through us and into the lives of others as God desires.

All of this ties together. It doesn't matter if we have entrepreneurial dreams or not... we must all strive to live in such a way, that when people see our lives, they see the representation of God in every aspect. King Solomon taught us in Ecclesiastes 9:10 (KJV), "Whatsoever thy hand findeth to do, do it with thy might; for there is no work, nor device, nor knowledge, nor wisdom, in the grave, whither thou goest."

In closing, I have come to realize that sometimes God shows up unexpectedly and whispers to us, "It's time to go higher. You've been around this mountain long enough." It reminds me of the Bible passage when the Lord said, "Ye have compassed this mountain long enough" (Deuteronomy 2:3 KJV).

And like faithful servants of God, we start packing some of our belongings. We look around at all that seems familiar as we prepare to elevate once again, into unfamiliar territories of greater faith. We climb inside His helicopter, and sometimes with tears in our eyes, we have to wave goodbye as we detach from old patterns and limiting beliefs. It is a beautiful price to pay, because nothing in all creation is of greater value than experiencing a close, intimate relationship with our Father in heaven.

So what exactly is the price of elevation and how much will it cost you?

The answer is nothing... and everything.

Nothing, because Jesus Christ [Yeshua] already went ahead of us all and paid the price in full. And everything, because all He asks for in return, is ALL of us (Romans 5:8, 1 Peter 2:24, Galatians 3:13, Deuteronomy 6:5, John 14:15, Luke 9:23)!

Reflection:

This was a tough chapter because it is one that will never end. God consistently calls us all to higher grounds, and we must get comfortable being uncomfortable as we pay the price of elevation by throwing off everything that hinders us, and running the race marked out for us (Hebrews 12:1-3).

Not everyone is willing to pay the price of elevation by going deeper in their walk with God and trusting His will for their lives. Not everyone is willing to pay this price because it requires a level of humility and commitment that cannot be substituted. I can only tell you, with all sincerity, it is a price I will pay for the rest of my life because walking in the will of God is what gives me life!

necessary.

Recommended Reading:

- *But those who hope in the LORD will renew their strength. They will soar on wings like eagles; they will run and not grow weary, they will walk and not be faint* (Isaiah 40: 31 NIV).
- *Behold, I am sending you out as sheep in the midst of wolves, so be wise as serpents and innocent as doves"* (Matthew 10:16 ESV).
- *Enter by the narrow gate. For the gate is wide and the way is easy that leads to destruction, and those who enter by it are many. For the gate is narrow and the way is hard that leads to life, and those who find it are few* (Matthew 7:13-14 ESV).
- *You will seek me and find me when you seek me with all your heart* (Jeremiah 29:13 NIV).
- Read Matthew 16:24-27 and examine what Jesus teaches about denying ourselves and following Him.

Assignment:

Spend some time in meditation and prayer before answering the questions below and moving on to the next chapter. It is important that you take time to evaluate your life and give careful thought to the decisions you wish to make as you move forward.

The Price of Elevation

1. What have you learned about developing a deeper relationship with God?

2. Can you identify areas of your life where God has called you to detach and go higher? If so, please clarify:

[Audio/Video version of this book is available at ZenjaGlass.com]

Chapter 16

Affirmation – Thank Your Naysayers!

To all my naysayers:

Thank you for all the thorns you placed in my paths.

Your pain forced me to new routes that led to my victories.

And thank you for the times you celebrated my defeats.

It led me into the arms of my Father

Where I found the strength to stand and continue on.

Everything you did to harm me

Turned out for my good.

I'm not even mad at you.

I'm not mad at all.

In fact, I want to thank you

Because you helped me to realize

There is greatness inside of me!

And I am highly favored by God!

[Audio/Video version of this book is available at ZenjaGlass.com]

Chapter 16

Thank Your Naysayers!

Sometimes you just need to take a moment to thank your naysayers because haters can be your greatest confirmations in life. They serve a valuable purpose to vet you and keep you on track by doing their best to test your authenticity and your strength to keep going. They are the reason the word tenacity is in the dictionary!

Are you determined enough, and dare I say, faithful enough to keep going, even when all odds are stacked against you? Even when your naysayers are louder than those who cheer for you?

We should be thankful for our naysayers because they help us build the spiritual muscles we need to maintain and handle the pressure at the level God is preparing us for.

Allow me to explain:

I am greatly encouraged by the story of Nehemiah in chapters 1-6 because it details all that happened in the 52 days it took to rebuild the wall of Jerusalem. From the onset, there was great opposition not only from their enemies but also from some of them who grew tired and became discouraged because the project seemed almost impossible to complete.

In Nehemiah 4:3 (NIV), one of the men said, "What they are building- even a fox climbing up on it would break down their wall of stones!" Then, in verses 6-8, people began plotting to fight against them as they saw the gaps were being closed on the wall and it was reaching about half its completed height. Throughout

necessary.

all of this, Nehemiah continued to encourage them to pray to God and continue with the work as he posted a guard day and night to help protect them (Nehemiah 4:9).

In Nehemiah 4:10, the strength of the laborers started giving out, and their enemies said, "Before they know it or see us, we will be right there among them and will kill them and put an end to the work" (Nehemiah 4:11 NIV). As if that wasn't enough opposition from naysayers and enemies, the workers were constantly being warned over and over again, "Wherever you turn, they will attack us" (Nehemiah 4:12 NIV). Nehemiah again told them, "Don't be afraid of them. Remember the Lord, who is great and awesome" (Nehemiah 4:14 NIV). He went on to encourage them to fight for their families and divided up the crew so that half of the men guarded the wall while the other half continued to build (Nehemiah 4:16-18). They stayed focused on what God had told them to do, despite all the opposition.

If you continue reading through chapters 5 and 6 you will see that there were many distractions that came their way in an attempt to stop them from building the wall. In fact, in Nehemiah 6:11-13, Nehemiah realized that someone was actually hired to intimidate him so that he would quit rebuilding the wall. Over and over again Nehemiah and the people had to pray to God to strengthen their hands and protect them so that they could remain focused and complete the building of the wall of Jerusalem.

And finally, in Nehemiah 6:15 (NIV) it states, "So the wall was completed on the twenty-fifth of Elul, in fifty-two days. When all our enemies heard about this, all the surrounding nations were afraid and lost their self-confidence, because they realized that this work had been done with the help of our God."

This is such an amazing Bible story for us to draw from when we have our sight set on a mission or a dream God has given us.

Thank Your Naysayers!

I have come to accept that opposition in my life serves a mighty purpose. In many cases, God has shown me that opposition confirms I am on the right track. The enemy comes to steal, kill, and destroy (John 10:10 NIV). And when I am working on an important project, especially one that aligns with walking in obedience to something God has placed in my heart to do, I can almost time it like clockwork when the oppositions will start to arise.

I want to challenge the way you view oppositions and hardships. Opposition is not always a punishment. Sometimes, it lights the very fire we need inside of us to move forth with faith, speed, and determination. In fact, I look for it as a confirmation, because the enemy is really not that creative. He tends to follow the same systems and patterns in our lives to keep us from moving forward.

For example, throughout the entire process of writing this book, several oppositions came my way, especially as I got closer to completing it... unexpected disagreements in my family, discord with my staff, financial concerns with the economy, random emergencies and situations that normally would not happen, and so forth. The more the opposition came, the more I prayed for God to show me how to turn it into gold, and use it for His good will. That is why you are reading about this right now. That opposition forced me to realize that my book must be a powerful threat to the enemy, and I must stay focused on completing what God told me to do.

We must keep our eyes open to what is happening in the Spirit, and not just in the physical realm. The Bible teaches us: "For our struggle is not against flesh and blood, but against the rulers, against the authorities, against the powers of this dark world and against the spiritual forces of evil in the heavenly realms" (Ephesians 6:12 NIV). The question is, do we really believe that?

necessary.

If we really believe this scripture to be true, then our lives should show it by how we respond when the opposition presents itself. When the naysayers appear, we shall rejoice because they are our confirmations that we are doing something of great importance! When God has told us to build a wall, and the opposition arises, we shall continue building and not be distracted by their presence. In fact, whenever we walk in alignment with God, we shall not be dismayed by the presence of our enemies because their very presence validates their fear of us achieving great things that will bring glory and honor to God. So I say to you my dear brothers and sisters, keep on building!

Don't stop because things are tough. Don't stop because people are talking about you. Don't stop because they mock what it looks like now. And please don't stop because you are afraid the dream is too big for you. Psalm 91 is a powerful Psalm to read if you are afraid. I pray you spend some time meditating on that Psalm as you sing songs of worship and praises to God, and continue with the mission He has given you.

We respond with confidence and joy because as children of God, our opposition is always an opportunity to learn, grow, and dare I say, pivot to something greater. Instead of getting mad at our naysayers, we should inwardly thank them for validating our importance in the spiritual realm. And if you have been forced to stop a project, or head in a different direction, don't be dismayed by that. Some of my best opportunities were discovered when I was forced to turn around and chart a new path because doors were closed and opposition prevented me from going in a certain direction. While I was discouraged in the moment, God quickly showed me it was a blessing in disguise. God can use any situation that comes against us to protect us, and reposition us for greener pastures!

Thank Your Naysayers!

God has proven time and time again that "No weapon that is formed against thee shall prosper" (Isaiah 54:17 KJV), and "All things work together for good to them that love God, to them who are the called according to his purpose" (Romans 8:28 KJV). This is why we are able to thank our naysayers and pray for those who oppose us, because they don't realize that it is a losing battle to oppose our God, who dwells in us!

The enemy doesn't realize that when he closes a door and sends words of discouragement, we will not relent. We will do exactly what Nehemiah did! We will continue the building we were assigned to do and not allow anyone, not even those from our own camps, to discourage us or distract us from moving forward.

So I say to you who are feeling tired, who are facing opposition from all sides, and who are tempted to lay down your tools and say, "Well Lord, I give up! I tried!" Don't give up! Unless God has made it clear to you, don't ever stop building the wall God has assigned for you to build.

Please consider that perhaps the opposition you are facing is your confirmation! I encourage you to pray in the Spirit on all occasions and imitate Nehemiah by continuing to work with one hand, and stand guard with your sword of the Spirit, which is the word of God, in the other hand (Ephesians 6:17)... and keep on building!

To God be all the glory!

Reflection:

As I look back over my life, I can truly say that my naysayers were some of my greatest gifts. They showed me that I had tremendous value because I was important enough to gain their

necessary.

negative attention. They proved to me that I was a threat to how they viewed themselves because they mocked my efforts and did their best to discourage me. They helped me to see that my Father was able to make a way out of no way when they withheld their support and anticipated my downfalls.

I sincerely thank them because they not only validated my authenticity, but they also served as guides by blocking pathways, which forced me to turn around, and head in the right direction.

And most importantly, I thank my naysayers because their pain forced me to run into the arms of God, where I found great strength and was molded to become His vessel!

Recommended Reading:

If you have time, I would love for you to read Nehemiah 1-6 so that you can see all the opposition he endured to remain faithful, focused, and complete the building of the wall of Jerusalem.

Then, read all of Psalm 91 for tremendous encouragement about how God will rescue and protect you.

Assignment:

1. Can you relate to Nehemiah? If so, how?

2. What decision(s) will you make to overcome the opposition you are facing?

Chapter 17

Affirmation – REST

I will no longer feel guilty for taking the time to REST.

I deserve me.

I deserve to be mentally and physically healthy.

I deserve to slow down and remember that I am alive.

Somehow, in the midst of taking care of others

I forgot to take care of me.

Starting today, I am going to take better care of myself.

And I won't allow anyone or anything

To make me feel badly about that.

I deserve to take care of me.

I deserve to rest.

[Audio/Video version of this book is available at ZenjaGlass.com]

Chapter 17

REST

Sometimes we don't realize we have been in survival mode for many years, because we never take the time to stop running and actually rest.

Why is it so difficult for us to rest?

And why do some of us feel guilty when we take time for ourselves, even when nothing at all is planned? It's as if we feel we are doing something wrong or perhaps missing out on something if we focus on resting and shutting down all the distractions life throws our way.

You might be surprised to know that God rested as well. The book of Genesis teaches us that after God formed the earth in six days and created all that was within it, He rested.

"Thus the heavens and the earth were finished, and all the host of them. And on the seventh day God ended his work which he had made; and he rested on the seventh day from all his work which he had made. And God blessed the seventh day, and sanctified it: because that in it he had rested from all his work which God created and made" (Genesis 2:1-3 KJV).

In fact, rest is actually one of the ten commandments given to Moses by God. God created a pattern of work and rest. Exodus 20:10 (KJV) states: "But the seventh day is the sabbath of the LORD thy God: in it thou shalt not do any work."

I won't begin to try to convince you one way or the other to honor the Sabbath because statistics show that the world is greatly

necessary.

divided on this subject. Some people believe we absolutely must continue to honor the Sabbath because it is one of the ten commandments, while others believe it is not necessary because that was Old Testament teaching. And if I can be very transparent, I am just now beginning to develop my own convictions about the importance of taking time to rest.

So I will approach it from this angle. Take away all the legalism and religious arguments, and simply ask yourself this question: Would it hurt to take some time out of each week to rest and take care of yourself mentally and physically by unplugging from all the busyness society brings so that you can have a day to reflect, reset, and rest?

Before you answer that question, let me share with you a few things I found out, not only from a sermon my minister recently preached, but also from my research. Did you know that people who take one day out of their week to rest live many years longer than others? Take some time to research this for yourself and you will see this has been proven in several research studies and among several religions that practice the Sabbath.

We must ask ourselves, why is that?

There are overwhelming statistics that show people throughout the world have extremely high levels of stress and anxiety in their lives now. I don't think any of us would find that difficult to believe because nowadays it is rare for someone not to feel stressed about life, their children, jobs, the economy, etc.

Whether you believe in honoring the Sabbath or not, do you think God was on to something? If the maker of the world took a day to rest, could it be possible that we are designed to do the same thing?

Could it be possible that God wants us to rest and give Him thanks? Could it be possible that He knows what is best for us physically and spiritually, and taking more time to rest is a part of His plan for our lives so that we can seek His guidance and thrive?

Could it be possible that He wants us to take a moment from the worries of life, and sit down to reflect and appreciate what was accomplished? Could it be possible that He wants us to take some time to notice His beautiful creation and admire all that He made for us?

In my humble opinion, we were never designed to constantly be distracted by all the pressures and technology the world brings our way. And I will be the first to admit that this is an area of my life that I struggle with at times because even though my children are adults now, I still have to force myself to slow down and not become distracted and consumed by the rush of life and all the responsibilities that come with it. Many years ago, I learned the hard way that stress can have a huge impact on our bodies, and it is so important that we take the time to rest.

When I was busy running all over the place, working hard and constantly taking care of others while neglecting my health, I didn't consider the impact it was having on my relationship with God, nor did I consider the impact it was having on my body. I became more irritable, my hair started falling out, I started getting stomach aches and headaches all the time, and though once a runner in my younger years, I could not run one single block without feeling like I was going to pass out!

To make matters worse, even when I went to sleep, my mind was always racing because I was either downloading all that happened that day or planning what I needed to get done the next day. And yes, I still prayed, read my Bible, went to church every Sunday, and so on, but I wasn't doing well.

I never allowed myself to fully rest. And the few times I was able to sleep in on a weekend, which was always a rare occasion, I still

necessary.

woke up feeling unrested because I was constantly being pulled in several directions at one time.

Can anyone relate to this?

I do not believe we were designed to run nonstop like robots, without taking time to simply rest, but like many of you, I had a lot on my plate. I felt like I couldn't slow down my pace because if I did that, certain things wouldn't get done; or at least, not to my standards. So, I did what many people do who have a tremendous number of responsibilities on their plate. I kept going... full-speed ahead!

My breaking point was when I went to my dentist and she told me that several of my teeth were severely chipped or completely broken in half! In fact, several had to be extracted! She asked if I was stressed. I jokingly replied, "Well, who isn't?" She went on to tell me that stress is a huge factor and that I was probably grinding my teeth throughout the night. She suggested that I start wearing a mouth guard so I wouldn't shatter any more teeth. I told her that I didn't grind my teeth and she had to be mistaken, but I took the mouth guard home anyway and wore it just to prove her wrong.

In less than a few days, that mouth guard was completely destroyed! I literally chewed through it and had to get a professional mouth guard made that would withstand the pressure from my intense grinding when I slept. I could not believe the amount of pressure my body was trying to cope with. It took me losing several teeth and undergoing several root canals before I finally began to wake up and realize what I was doing to myself.

During that time, I remember meeting with a licensed professional counselor for several weeks just to discuss my life and perhaps point out my blind spots so that I could take better care of my mental, physical, and spiritual well-being. I will never forget my first session with her. She asked me if I noticed the freshly cut blades of grass on the ground and the new buds that were flowering near the door before I entered the building. I couldn't tell her whether there was grass on the ground or if it was just concrete pavement! And I certainly could not tell her if a single flowering bud was on any tree, because I didn't see any trees or plants. All I saw were the pressures of life and all the things I had on my plate that needed to get accomplished that day.

I learned some very valuable lessons from those sessions. I learned I needed to slow down. I needed to rest. I was simply rushing through life, and missing out on noticing and appreciating the journey. I was so busy trying to do what I thought were the right things to do by being responsible, providing for my family, and taking care of others, that I didn't realize I deserved to take care of myself as well... without feeling guilty about it. I had a right to say no to others without any excuse, even if I had nothing else planned except to stare out my window and take notice of the beautiful trees and freshly cut blades of grass.

I had a right to rest, and I needed to give myself permission to live before I die. Because, whether we accept this or not, life is just a mist (James 4:14). We are here and gone in the blink of an eye. And when we do not take the time to be present because we are so consumed with the busyness of life, in my opinion, it is as if we are rushing... to die.

Why did I take the time to share all of this? Because I care about your overall well-being, and most importantly, God cares. It took a scary trip to the ER one day when my chest was hurting, for me to finally wake up and make some major changes in my life. When the hospital ran all their tests and said it must be stress because everything looked fine to them, I knew something had to change. I was slowly running myself into the ground because I had no off button to slow me down. So God had to do it for me!

necessary.

Between the headaches, broken teeth, lack of sleep, constant stress, chest pain, and I won't even mention bad eating habits, I had to make some significant changes.

That is around the time I started going far deeper in my relationship with God by sitting in my closet every night just to pray and be silent in His presence. Then, I started reserving Friday evening to Saturday evening to listen to sermons, meditate on the word of God, and play worship music as I sang praises to God. And it is not as if someone told me I must do that. I simply made that decision after hearing a lesson taught by one of the elders at my church about the importance of the Sabbath and learning from God by taking the time to rest. I thought to myself, *I have never done that before, but what harm could it bring? In fact, I need it!*

To make a long story very short, my mental, physical, and spiritual health improved dramatically because I started taking actions to get the help I needed in every area of my life. Most importantly, I renewed my commitment to deepen my relationship with God, and I learned how to slow down, even in the midst of fires.

The more time I spent sitting with God and giving Him my full attention, the more peace and wisdom came into my life because I wasn't running around in chaos trying to keep several plates spinning at one time. Now, I make it a point to listen to a sermon, meditate on the word of God, and pray before going to bed almost every night because it calms my spirit and I rest peacefully when I am filled with His presence. I can't begin to tell you how much my life has changed as a result. God has given me wisdom in areas that have changed the entire trajectory of my life. And in case you are wondering, my teeth are no longer breaking!

I won't dare say I have arrived because finding rest is a journey for me. I have been working since I was 13 years old, so it is very difficult for me to slow down and actually rest. And it wasn't until I entered my 50s, that I began to realize that throughout most of my life I was always running in survival mode. I never really took the time to rest and allow myself to be fully present.

In fact, in the next chapter you are about to read, you will discover some very painful childhood memories that I tucked far away for most of my life. It wasn't until I started the process of sitting with God and learning to rest, that I began to realize I was running from so much pain throughout my life. I didn't even know I was in survival mode, until God slowly took me by the hand, and gave me permission to rest in Him.

Regardless of your religious beliefs, I believe there is a lesson we can all learn from the maker of heaven and earth. He worked for six days, and on the seventh day, the maker of the universe, the omnipotent (all powerful), the omniscient (all-knowing), and omnipresent (present everywhere) God [Yahweh, YHWH] actually... RESTED!

My gentle challenge for you is to simply REST. Take time to slow down, and rest in the presence of God, and give thanks to Him.

Trust that He will take care of things... and rest!

Lay all your burdens down before Him... and rest!

And after you have done all that you know to do, sit in His presence... and rest!

Reflection:

I pray that we all live before we die. And part of living is resting. I am finally learning the importance of taking the time to rest. There is certainly nothing wrong with pursuing the dreams God

necessary.

planted inside of us, and striving to go to higher levels because God built us to serve Him and to thrive, but we must never forget the importance of taking care of ourselves mentally, physically, and spiritually.

Consider this important question: What good would it be to finally arrive wherever your "there" is, and because you never rested, you can't even enjoy it?

Recommended Reading:

- *Yes, my soul, find rest in God; my hope comes from him. Truly he is my rock and my salvation; he is my fortress, I will not be shaken* (Psalm 62:5-6 NIV).
- *Do not be wise in your own eyes; fear the LORD and shun evil. This will bring health to your body and nourishment to your bones* (Proverbs 3:7-8 NIV).
- *Come to me, all you who are weary and burdened, and I will give you rest. Take my yoke upon you and learn from me, for I am gentle and humble in heart, and you will find rest for your souls. For my yoke is easy and my burden is light* (Matthew 11:28-30 NIV).

Assignment:

1. Why do you think God rested? What can you learn from Him?

2. Reevaluate your schedule and develop a plan to have some downtime every day, even if it is only for a few minutes to pray and read your Bible.

REST

3. If you are willing, develop a detailed plan to set aside one day a week to rest and spend time alone with God.

[Audio/Video version of this book is available at ZenjaGlass.com]

Chapter 18

Affirmation – Horseback Ride

I forgive myself.

I made the best decisions I knew to make

With the wisdom, knowledge, and courage I had at that time.

But now, I am wiser. I am stronger!

And what happened in the past

Shall never happen again!

I won't feel guilty for what I didn't know.

I won't feel discouraged because I wasn't strong enough.

I won't be angry with myself any longer.

I've moved on to higher grounds.

And what happened in my past shall hinder me no more.

I forgive myself.

I forgive me.

And now, I am ready to live!

[Audio/Video version of this book is available at ZenjaGlass.com]

Chapter 18

Horseback Ride

I only wanted a horseback ride. I never knew it would change my life forever.

He was no stranger to the family. He was completely drunk, as was the norm during that time, but I had no reason to turn down a moment of happiness by accepting his horseback ride. It was finally my turn, and I was so excited! So without hesitation, I jumped into his arms and swirled around to his back so that I could ride like the other kids and enjoy being a cowgirl.

He bucked and galloped around the room, and trotted like a horse with me on his back, skipping, and making funny sounds while I held on tight. It was so much fun! I laughed and laughed, as he galloped around the living room, staggering into almost every piece of furniture, but I didn't care because I was a cowgirl and it was exciting being lifted high into the air and spinning around the room.

Little did I know, my laughter would be short-lived.

As he galloped me around the room, he put both of his arms behind his back, under my dress, and firmly held my bottom. I paid little attention to that because I thought he was simply trying to keep me from falling lower on his back. I thought he was providing a sort of seat for me, only with his hands, to keep me secured. Then, without any warning, I felt his fingers quickly maneuvering through my panties and inserting through a part of my body that was never touched. I didn't know what was happening. It was as if the horseback ride came to a slow,

necessary.

grinding end, as he began to violate me in ways a young child should never experience. He had no right to rob me of freedom, as he jumped around the room, forcing his way into my body, ignoring my pleas to put me down. For some reason I couldn't scream for help, even though my mother was only a few feet away. I can still recall the smell of the fried catfish my mother was cooking in the kitchen while he galloped me around the living room – drunk, staggering over furniture, and robbing me of my innocence.

For the first time in my life, my eyes were opened to a demonic spirit I never knew existed. I didn't realize an adult could do that to a child. I didn't scream. I didn't yell. I just kept saying, "I want to get down now. Put me down." It was the only gentle plea I could muster because I was in a state of pain, shock, confusion, and for some reason, embarrassment as though I did something wrong.

He laughed it off, and eventually lowered me down to the floor. And no sooner than my feet could touch the floor, I quickly ran into my bedroom and shut the door… never saying a word to anyone.

I sat in my room. Throbbing in areas never touched. Robbed. Confused. Feeling unprotected. And for some reason, ashamed. And forever changed.

I don't recall eating dinner that night, but I do recall thinking to myself that I didn't want to cause any trouble and ruin the little bit of happiness I saw in my mother's face as she made dinner. I also didn't want him to beat my mother because I knew if I told her what just happened, she would have come to my defense. So I protected her. I said nothing. I kept my momma safe. I kept my siblings safe. Somehow, as young as I was, I reasoned that by keeping silent and pretending nothing happened, I was protecting my family. I don't even know if he remembered what happened by the next day. He acted as if all was well, but I was forever changed. I stayed silent. I took the fall for the family, for the sake of one less argument... one less move... one less traumatic event. My mother has now passed away. I never told her what happened that day.

I can't count the number of times I stood up to abusers in my momma's life from such a young age. Perhaps that's why they tried to avoid fighting her directly in front of me, because they knew I would grab a mirror, or anything my small hands could hold, and run to her defense. But that time, the abuse was directed at me. It took me by surprise, and the little warrior inside of me was just beginning to rise.

My mother was a young teenager when she gave birth to me. Unfortunately, her mother passed away as a young woman. And without much guidance from a mother figure in her life, it was no surprise my momma became pregnant at a very young age, after one experience with a man in the military who wanted to meet her in the back of a truck on a warm fall day.

In essence, she was a child raising a child, and she did her very best to raise her children with the wisdom and courage she had at that time. After my mother gave birth to me, she discovered one of my aunts had already named me Zenja, pronounced "Zen-Jah." My momma could never pronounce my name. The best she could say was some form of "Zen-Yah."

Despite the fact that she was constantly in and out of abusive relationships in her younger years, she was a very loving mother who always taught her children about God. She had a huge heart and would always find a way to give to others. I would not have traded my mother for anyone in the world. She loved hard, and everyone knew it. Many years later, my mom not only became a licensed social worker, but a licensed minister as well.

necessary.

In case you are wondering about my biological father, I will give you some brief details that you might find puzzling to believe:

My biological father lived only a few blocks away from us; however, I never met him while growing up, nor did I ever see his face as a child... not even a photo! When he returned from the military, he married someone and started a family. To my understanding, my father did not get involved in my life because he didn't want to fight with the men in my mother's life. I don't think that's a valid reason to stay out of a child's life, but that is what I was told.

As a child, I would often ride my bike past his house just to see my last name on his mailbox. I remember it like it was yesterday. I would quickly ride my little bike up to his house, pause, and just stare at my last name that was painted on the side of his mailbox. I always hoped that one day he would come to the door, or be present in the yard, just so that I could see his face. I just wanted to know what he looked like. It may seem strange for me to say this, but as a child, with so much turmoil happening in my life, it felt good to know that there was a secure place that had my name on it. It felt good to know that my name was on my father's house. That day never arrived until many years later, when I was a young adult in college, and received a phone call from him after a relative gave him my phone number. Since then, by the grace of God, we have developed a wonderful relationship.

As I reflect on my shaping years, I recall another adult friend of the family who attempted something I will never forget. I was at my grandfather's house, where I felt the safest, when that demon approached our front door.

My grandfather was instrumental in helping to raise me from a baby until my pre-teen years, before we eventually moved up North. Not only was he a Baptist minister, but he was one of the most gifted carpenters you could find. He would build a house or

Horseback Ride

a church building without ever holding a blueprint in his hand. All he needed was his wooden pencil that he kept in his front pocket, a ruler, his tobacco, and a six-pack of beer!

During my younger years, I would always visit my grandpa. Many times, I would stay for weeks, or even months at his house, and I loved it! My younger sister and I would spend the entire day loading wood in his shed, just to earn a quarter so that we could run to the store and buy 25 pieces of gum and candy. Those were the days!

At any time, you could find me in his garden, loading wood in his stove, preserving jam and homemade pickles in mason jars, feeding the chickens, making ice cream out of snow with him, or sitting in the church pews, watching him preach his sermons every Sunday morning. I would not hesitate to run up to him, in the middle of his lesson, and stand by his side as the congregation smiled while he continued to preach a powerful sermon. I would even find my way to the choir and lead some old gospel songs while he smiled from ear to ear, watching his young granddaughter sing praises to the Lord.

On one particular summer day, grandpa was in the backyard, picking vegetables from his garden, and I was in the house alone. Then, a friend of my uncle, who was probably in his early 20s, showed up at the front door and asked where my uncle was. I told him my uncle was down the street and would be back in a little bit. Instead of waiting outside, he immediately entered the house and looked out the back window to make sure my grandpa was in the garden. He quickly started telling me to lay down on the couch so that he could get on top of me and make me feel good. He said it wouldn't hurt and would only take a few minutes.

I remember saying no several times as he motioned me to the couch. I was only a little girl, but I recognized the demon in his eyes, and even though I didn't understand all that he wanted to

necessary.

do, I knew it was wrong and I needed to get out of that room. He kept looking out the back window to make sure my grandpa was still in the garden as he kept prompting me to lay down on the couch. He kept telling me he would make me feel good, but he had no idea how that moment forever changed my life. I don't think it is necessary to go into too much detail about what happened, but I will say, it was only by the grace of God, that just before he was able to complete his evil intent, we heard my uncle talking as he was approaching the front door.

His friend quickly ran outside and acted as if nothing happened. They sat in the front yard, enjoying a drink, having lively discussions as they always did. I distinctly remember making the decision that I would not say anything to my grandpa nor my uncle about what just happened because I knew they loved me dearly, and I also knew my uncle would seriously hurt anyone who tried to harm his family.

I had witnessed my uncle on many occasions beat down the men who beat my mother. He was a skinny man, and one of his legs was shorter than the other, so he walked with a limp. But he had a powerful punch and he kept a shovel in the back of his car to beat anyone he had altercations with.

My uncle was a hot-tempered man, and the entire town knew it, but he loved his family deeply. He was the kind of uncle who would completely curse me out if I gave him any money as a holiday or birthday gift because he felt it was his job to take care of his nieces and nephews, not the other way around. I learned that lesson the hard way!

So I sat there, completely broken in spirit, confused, feeling unprotected, and staring out the window, observing that demon sitting next to my uncle under the oak tree as he enjoyed a cold bottle of Coca-Cola. Without a doubt in my mind, I knew if my uncle was aware of what his friend had just attempted to do, he would have killed him.

So I remained silent. I didn't want my words to kill anyone.

Reflection:

These events happened in my life when I was just a little girl, prior to us fleeing up North from an abusive relationship. This is why resting is so important. When I finally began to take the time to rest, and sit silently with God, it allowed me the necessary time I needed to remember… and to heal.

I have gone back to those places with God and received the healing I needed, but I chose to keep this chapter in my book because I know that a large percentage of people can probably identify in some way or another. And in case you are wondering, my uncle has since then passed away. He never knew what happened.

It is easy to ask someone why they didn't say anything after the abuse occurred. I am not a professional counselor and I won't pretend to speak on behalf of others. As for myself, I simply did not know what to do at that time. I did not have the wisdom nor the courage to make a different choice. I forgive myself for what I did not know, and I pray that somehow, by including this chapter in my book, the cycle of remaining silent is prevented and healing is provided for others. If only one person has been helped by my story, it is well worth it!

necessary.

Recommended Reading:

I'd like to do something a little different. Instead of a recommended reading, I would like to ask you to check on those you love and let them know you are there for them if they ever have anything they want to talk about that might seem uncomfortable. Please also take some time to pray for those who are dealing with abusive situations.

Additionally, check on yourself. If you can identify with any area of my story, please know you are not alone. There are several communities and organizations throughout the world that are willing to help you.

I pray if there is anyone who is going through this right now or who has not come forth to get help (especially a child, teenager, or young adult), that you would please find someone to speak with. I will be providing resources to nationally recognized organizations on my website under the Resources/Help tab at www.ZenjaGlass.com.

I love you all.

Z.

Assignment:

1. Can you identify with any part of this chapter? If so, how?

2. Have you begun the journey of healing from within? If not, what steps are you willing to take... to take care of you?

Chapter 19

Affirmation – You Are a Lion!

Who is this that I see?

I don't recognize you anymore.

You walk with a different stride

As though you are a lion!

You walk as if you know

You are fiercely and wonderfully made.

As if you know you can do anything!

Ah, now I see where your confidence arises.

Now I see why you achieve what seems impossible to others.

I see the King of kings in your shadow!

I see the lion standing next to you.

I see the lion… in you!

[Audio/Video version of this book is available at ZenjaGlass.com]

Chapter 19

You Are a Lion!

I will never forget many years ago when my daughter, who is now an adult, was in middle school, and I found her crying in her room because some girls at her school didn't want to talk to her anymore. She sobbed about having done nothing wrong and she didn't understand why all of a sudden they turned against her. She was so heartbroken. She could barely speak as she cried, while saying, "I don't understand why they won't talk to me. I didn't do anything to them." She went on and on about how they gave her the silent treatment. She was truly crushed. You could see even from her body language that she was very dependent on those relationships, and she placed her happiness in their hands. I had never seen her become so distraught and cry so hard!

I am sure most mothers would have sympathized, held their daughters, and told them everything was going to be OK. But in that moment, something inside of me sparked. It was a righteous anger because it took everything in me to sit still as I watched this beautiful, kind-hearted, loving young girl allow her self-confidence to be shattered by the thoughts and opinions of others. So without any pre-planned speech, I began to give her wisdom that poured out from the depth of my soul. To this day, that was a moment she told me she would NEVER forget because it completely changed her life!

I closed her door and got about two inches away from her face. I looked her straight in the eyes and said:

necessary.

"You are a LION! You are a lion because my blood flows through your veins, and the blood [the Spirit] of Jesus Christ flows through me. I am a LION, and the power that is within me has been passed on to you. That power is the strength of God! Don't ever beg someone to love you or accept you! Lions sometimes have to walk alone. Lions lead the way. Lions are courageous. Lions are powerful! And you are powerful because of the God that we serve. You are boldly and fiercely made! Things that would devour most people, do not devour us because He that is within us is greater than He that is in the world. When people know that their rejection can crush you, they will continue to use that power over you. Don't ever give your power away! So I want you to go to school and walk with your head held high because you know who you are! Don't run after people! Run after knowing who you are... a beautiful, powerful LION in God! Don't ever be afraid to walk alone, sit alone, or make new friends. Others will become attracted to the light they see in you. I am a lion! And you are my child! My blood flows through you. Don't you EVER forget who you are... You are a LION!"

As I spoke those words to my tender young daughter, her eyes widened, her facial expression completely changed, and she was empowered because for the first time in her life, she knew who she was! She walked in her school the next day with her head held high. She later told me that she sat by herself in the cafeteria the next day, with no fears of being alone, and with a newfound confidence that she never had. She made new friends and never again allowed anyone to define her self-worth or demean her value.

Now, some of you might be thinking that was a bit too much to tell a young girl who was simply crying about lost friendships because that is a normal part of life, and it happens all the time in school. But I would like to tell you this: From that day forth, my daughter never had that issue again because she knew who she was... a lion! For the first time in her life, she understood the power in knowing what she was made of and where she comes from. And while this story is probably a typical scenario that occurs in our children's lives, I think it is critical that they start to learn, as young as possible, that they are enough, and no one gets to determine their value and rule over them in such a way that they beg for acceptance from others!

For me, that issue was larger than simply a lost friendship, it was an identity issue. She needed to know who she was, and the power that lived inside of her. That was very important for her to learn so that she would not take those same insecurities into her adult life by letting others determine her value.

My daughter is an adult now, and to this day, she still remembers that precious moment when she realized the power that was already living inside of her. It was always there; she just didn't know it. Sometimes we have to be reminded of who we really are in the presence of God when we face our difficult times in life.

In fact, over the years there have been a few precious moments when she would call or text me saying: "Mom, I need to hear that lion story again." So, I would call or text her back, "My daughter, you are a LION. You are a lion because..." She would reply, "Thanks mom!"

I decided to share this private story with the world because it made such a huge impact in my daughter's life, and to my surprise, it tremendously impacted the lives of people in several nations after I shared this story on one of my podcast episodes titled "You Are a Lion."

necessary.

I did not expect so many people would find their story in the story of a child who was distraught over some friends talking about her and refusing to sit with her. But isn't it funny how God works in our lives? Sometimes we can find our answers in life by simply learning from children.

A common response I received from many of my podcast and social media subscribers was, "I wish I had someone in my life who told me those words when I was younger." It broke my heart to hear those words because, even though I had a very challenging childhood growing up in poverty, my momma always told me I was a lion. I remember when her health was rapidly declining and she could no longer speak, but she mouthed the words to me: "You are a lion. You are strong, baby. You are very strong!"

I broke down in tears because I didn't want her to leave me, nor did I believe I was strong enough to deal with all the pressures I was feeling at that time. I was shaking so hard. I placed my forehead on her forehead and I said, "Momma, please don't leave me. I'm not that strong. I'm not that strong momma!" I thought she would cry with me, but she didn't. She moved me about two or so inches from her face, looked me in the eyes with a determined, resolute, strong expression, without any fears or doubts about the words she was about to say, and she mouthed, "You are a lion! You are strong, baby! You strong! And you are going to make it!" She died a few hours later.

It took me some time to realize that the strength she was talking about was not only my strength in character and perseverance, but my strength in God. She would always tell me to be strong in the Lord. In that moment, when I was feeling powerless and weak, I discovered a new level of strength I didn't even know I had. I had been given the strength to stand and continue on because my momma reminded me of who I was... a lion in Christ!

If you have never been told these words, I want you to hear them now. I want you to hear and believe the very words my momma passed down to me, I passed down to my daughter, and now, am passing on to you:

"You are a lion! You are strong! You are strong, baby! You strong! And even when you don't believe you have the strength to go on, or the power to overcome whatever challenges are coming your way... even though no one may have told you this when you were younger, know that I am telling you now... YOU ARE A LION! YOU ARE STRONG! AND YOU WILL MAKE IT! Be strong in the Lord and in His mighty power!"

Please don't ever beg anyone to love you. Please don't ever beg anyone to accept you. If someone has decided to walk out of your life, I pray that God gives you the strength to walk in love, and in humility, as you open the door very wide... and wish them well.

If the season has come for some people to leave your life, you must know that sometimes you have to be OK with standing alone... just you and God. I am a living witness that sometimes our greatest growth comes from the lowest valleys, when we had to stand alone. Those were the times when God showed me that I was enough, and despite what others said about me, He saw the best in me!

You are a lion! You have something special to offer the world. And I sincerely pray that after reading or listening to this chapter, you walk with your head held a little bit higher, and

necessary.

you begin to elevate your thinking and place greater value on yourself.

You are a child of God! A fierce lion! And you can do anything through Christ who strengthens you!

This isn't arrogance talking. It's a knowing. A knowing of who you are... and whose you are. An heir of the King (Romans 8:17).

I sincerely pray you never forget this!

Reflection:

To this day, when I am tempted to be afraid or worry about any situation in life, I find myself going into my closet (which, by the way, is my secret place with God), and asking Him, "Tell me again who do you say I am? I am sorry I forgot. I need to be reminded again of who I am in your presence!"

Those are the exact words I say to God when I forget who I am. I also say those words when I start to rely on my own strength and forget what I am capable of achieving, or overcoming. Sometimes, I simply have to be reminded that I am a child of God (John 1:12) and nothing is impossible with Him (Luke 1:37).

Recommended Reading:

- *Do not weep! See, the Lion of the tribe of Judah, the Root of David, has triumphed* (Revelation 5:5 NIV).

- *We have come to know and have believed the love which God has for us* (1 John 4:16 NASB).
- *See what kind of love the Father has given to us, that we should be called children of God; and so we are* (1 John 3:1 ESV).

Assignment:

Take some time to read the recommended passages again and write a short paragraph on who you are in God. In other words, write how you believe God views you. Then, describe in detail what you believe He is capable of doing in your life.

[Audio/Video version of this book is available at ZenjaGlass.com]

Chapter 20

Affirmation – If Greatness Could Speak

I am sorry you had to endure many hardships
And dig deep valleys to find me.
For I do not lay atop the soil.

I waited patiently as I watched you search for me
In relationships, careers, and affirmations from others.

I am sorry you did not recognize me when you looked in the
Mirror and doubted yourself, your talents and your abilities.

I am sorry you did not hear my whispers
When you felt powerless.

I was there through every setback you experienced.
Every trial and tribulation.
Every painful, discouraging moment of your life.

And I was there when you didn't believe in yourself...

I was always there… waiting for you to discover me.

I was there when you felt you couldn't go another day.

I was there when everyone you thought you could depend on,

Turned around and walked away.

I wrapped myself around you and held you closely on the days

You felt the pain was unbearable.

I never let you go.

I never lost my grip.

And I never will.

At last, you have found me!

At last, you have discovered

I was always within you!

Chapter 20

If Greatness Could Speak

I thought I was supposed to stoop low and pretend greatness wasn't inside of me so others could feel good about themselves.

It didn't work.

Somehow, I thought I would receive more love and acceptance from others if I hid my gifts and talents, and remained less than who I was created to be.

That didn't work either.

So I hid greatness under a bowl. And only when no one was around, would I peek inside to see if her light was still burning.

She burned low for many years as she waited for me to develop the courage to let her shine.

I did my best to ignore her tantrums as I kept her hidden... out of sight... protected from criticism.

I knew if she ever fully came forth, and showed herself to the world, nothing would ever be the same because while her presence inspires many people, it also invites criticism and envy from naysayers and from those who choose to remain stagnant.

She challenges the status quo with no apologies! She not only changes the atmosphere wherever she goes, but you must change to remain in her presence.

Despite my best efforts to keep her hidden and locked away, her tantrums grew louder. Her desire to shine could no longer be

necessary.

tucked away. Greatness began to wrestle with me in the middle of the night by reminding me she was never created to remain hidden! And I was created to bring her forth!

As I sat in the presence of my Father, asking for guidance and purpose in my life, a fire began to burn inside of me, encouraging me to use my gifts and talents, and pleading with me to allow greatness to come forth without fear. I sought God's guidance for my life, as though I were searching for hidden treasure. For years, I spent countless hours in prayer, reading my Bible, worshipping God in song, and meditating on His words as I begged Him to rescue me from my tribulations and give me the wisdom and courage to pursue His will for my life.

The closer I drew to God, the more I realized I was living a life in fear of what others would say if I truly used the talents He gave me. God began to reveal that He had plans to prosper me and not to harm me (Jeremiah 29:11). He reminded me that I was predestined for His good will (Ephesians 1:11-12). He gave me the courage to step out in faith, and know that He will command his angels concerning me to direct my path (Psalm 91:11).

Little by little, I began to lift the bowl and let her light pierce through small openings... just big enough to light up the room when no one else was around. Her light began to shine brighter and brighter. Despite my best efforts to keep her hidden, her presence could no longer be ignored. Darkness could not detain her, and by the mighty grace of God and His favor on my life, I could no longer delay allowing her to come forth for the world to see.

I could no longer downplay my hopes and dreams. I could no longer be afraid of the treasures that come with embracing wisdom. I could no longer walk in fear of success because I was created to thrive and it was time for me to walk in the power, and in the authority my Father planted inside of me. It was time for me to remember who God created me to be, an heir of God (Romans 8:17)... a child of the Almighty God (1 John 3:1)!

I must admit, I felt a little guilty for accepting the greatness God put inside of me. From my observation, most people kept her safely tucked away, under a bowl, never to show her brightness to the world. So was I wrong to dare lift that bowl and allow her to shine? I asked this question because somehow, way in the back of my mind, I thought if I pursued the dreams God gave me, that would mean I was not grateful for all that God had done in my life. Pursuing greater goals and dreams initially made me feel as if I was either being worldly, putting dreams above taking care of my family, or complaining to God as if He hadn't blessed me enough.

God released me from those lies. I came to the realization that it would have been selfish of me to refuse to let God be glorified in my life, through the gifts and talents He planted inside of me. God knows, I often put myself last because I was always taking care of others. When the time came for me to respond to the call of greatness over my life, I had to realize I owed it to myself, my family, and to God, to go higher... and expect greater!

Yes, we should be grateful for every single thing God has done for us, but we must also never forget that greatness is who God is! He made us to reign, to walk in power and in His authority. His seeds of greatness are planted all throughout the Bible. And when we intently look into the word of God, there is a constant call to know God, be strong, and prosper (Daniel 11:32). It's a beautiful secret that we all must know and never forget!

When God gives us talents and plants a dream inside of us, He expects a return that glorifies Him. Perhaps that is why I love "The Parable of the Talents" (referred to as "The Parable of the Bags of Gold," in some Bible translations) in Matthew 25:14-30. It is such a beautiful parable that teaches us to use what God has

necessary.

given us, to multiply and produce a return on His investment in us, to serve Him. We should never bury His talents by walking in fear! As a seed must be buried and die to itself to produce more fruit (John 12:24), so we must follow the process and the plan of God in every area of our lives by growing and producing fruit that will last.

I think it is so important that we dive deeply into the word of God to get a healthy perspective of how God views wealth. As a Christian, I always thought that money, riches, and wealth were in some way, worldly and evil in the sight of God. Somehow, I believed if we ever put any focus on growing our economies, increasing our influence, and attaining riches of any kind, that would be totally ungodly because, after all, Jesus didn't pursue those things, and the Bible teaches us: "For the love of money is the root of all evil" (1 Timothy 6:10 KJV).

Did you catch that? It is the "love" of money that is the root of all evil. Somehow, throughout my entire life as a disciple of Jesus Christ, I missed that part!

And that's not all I missed. I missed a genuine understanding of what comes with wisdom. The Bible teaches us that "Long life is in her right hand; in her left hand are riches and honor" (Proverbs 3:16 NIV). The Bible also teaches us what becomes of the person whose delight is in the law of the Lord. It states, "And he shall be like a tree planted by the rivers of water, that bringeth forth his fruit in his season; his leaf also shall not wither; and whatsoever he doeth shall prosper" (Psalm 1:3 KJV). That passage should encourage us to know that God desires to prosper us!

Greatness is powerful! She brings action and attention from all nations. And if we are not careful, we can begin to worship gifts and treasures that were never meant to take the place of God in our lives. Below are two powerful passages I wrote on the tablet of my heart so that I would always remember to walk in wisdom as I pursued the dreams God planted inside of me.

- "Do not wear yourself out to get rich; do not trust your own cleverness" (Proverbs 23:4 NIV).
- "Do not store up for yourselves treasures on earth, where moths and vermin destroy, and where thieves break in and steal. But store up for yourselves treasures in heaven, where moths and vermin do not destroy, and where thieves do not break in and steal. For where your treasure is, there your heart will be also" (Matthew 6:19-21 NIV).

These are the pearls of wisdom that we must hold in our hands as we take courageous steps to unlocking greatness in our lives.

So there I was, answering to the cries of greatness because she refused to be hidden any longer. I had an obligation to myself, and to God, to lift that bowl and allow her to shine before the world. And oh my, did her light begin to shine!

I never knew greatness was such a threat to complacency.

I never knew greatness had enemies who were threatened by her very presence. But I could no longer hide her because she was predestined, and I was created to bring her forth!

Little did I know that her glow was too bright for most people to stay in the room. I didn't know her light would expose their dark, insecure places.

I didn't know her presence would make some people walk away.

I didn't know her presence attracted enemies and naysayers.

I didn't know her presence would change my appearance to reflect the image of my Father.

I didn't know her presence would be a gift to the world.

necessary.

I didn't know her presence would change the world!

Greatness never needed anyone's permission to do what she was created to do. She only needed to be released because she was predestined to do the will of God. If greatness could speak, what do you think she would be saying to you right now? And more importantly, are you willing to answer her call?

It is not something to consider lightly, because you are going to have to get used to being uncomfortable as you become a better version of yourself. You are going to have to get used to being misunderstood, because some people may not understand why you are pursuing that dream or goal. Some people may even try to talk you out of doing what God has told you to do.

And here is the good news: You can do this! You can do this because God has already gone ahead of you (Ephesians 1:11). He gave you those dreams, passions, and visions for a reason. I can only hope and pray that you commit your life to God, trust the Good Shepherd, and live your life to the fullest (John 10:10) as you bring glory and honor to God with your gifts and talents.

Listen closely and hear greatness whispering to you:

"Who is this person I now see with eyes wide open and chariots of horses of fire all around? You no longer relent in the presence of fear. You no longer heed to barriers. You stand in great might and sit at the table in the presence of your enemies. Your oil runneth over. Goodness and mercy follow you.

Who is this person having a great impact on the world, dwelling in the house of the Lord, robed in greatness?

It is you.

It is you!"

If Greatness Could Speak

Reflection:

I always thought I had to make a choice between being devoted to God and pursuing my dreams and being a leader in business or public sectors. Now I realize God needs His representation at all levels, on all platforms, and in all sectors to have influence and reach His people in every nation. I truly believe God desires to bless us and increase our territory (Jeremiah 29:11), and He is willing to put in us what He can get through us! Therefore, we must not be afraid to uncover greatness and bring her forth.

Greatness is knocking at your door. Will you let her enter?

Oh how I wish we would all let her shine brightly, so that we can light up the world together!

Recommended Reading:

- *You are the light of the world. A town built on a hill cannot be hidden. Neither do people light a lamp and put it under a bowl. Instead they put it on its stand, and it gives light to everyone in the house. In the same way, let your light shine before others, that they may see your good deeds and glorify your Father in heaven* (Matthew 5:14-16 NIV).

Assignment:

Let's have a little fun with this assignment. Take a moment to pause and go look in the mirror. Do you recognize who you see?

necessary.

Do you recognize Greatness is staring back at you? She is smiling because you are her reflection!

As you stare into your mirror, I want you to imagine you are the voice of greatness. Write what you think this voice would say to you. Be as detailed as possible. And if you are willing, pray to God for wisdom and insight about how to move forward.

Chapter 21

Affirmation – If I Were Your Enemy!

Response to Negativity:
You don't get to tell me that I am going to fail!
You don't get to tell me that I am not good enough!
I won't listen to you any longer…

I listen to my Father now.
He has revealed the truth to me.

I am GREATER than who you say I am!
And despite my past failures
I will be victorious!

You don't get to tell me that I will not soar!

All things are possible for me
Because I am a child of the Most High King!

[Audio/Video version of this book is available at ZenjaGlass.com]

Chapter 21

If I Were Your Enemy!

If I were your enemy, I would encourage you to doubt your God-given talents and abilities. I would tell you that you are always behind schedule so that you would be discouraged and abandon your dreams. I would never want you to read Joshua 1:9, Mark 10:27, or Galatians 6:9 because those scriptures would remind you to be courageous and never give up.

If I were your enemy, I would do everything possible to keep you from reading and understanding Revelation 1:6, Revelation 5:10, 1 Peter 2:9-10, Romans 8:17, Ephesians 3:6, and Galatians 3:29 because there is no way I would want you to know anything about the power that you have over me! I wouldn't want you knowing you are an heir of God, a co-heir with Jesus Christ, a royal priesthood who should live and command authority as priests and kings. There is no way you should know that!

If I were your enemy, I would keep you stuck in the past and constantly remind you of how everyone wronged you, so that you could never fully embrace the love of God or move forward in life. And I would never ever show you Jeremiah 29:11, because I wouldn't want you knowing that despite what happened, God has plans to prosper you. This way, you would remain living in the past instead of thriving in the future. That would make me very happy!

If I were your enemy, I would encourage you to be fearful of trying anything new or anything people could criticize you about. I would remind you of past failures when you are considering pursuing your dreams. And I would do my best to keep you from

necessary.

reading the scripture that states, "I can do all things through him who strengthens me" (Philippians 4:13 ESV). I wouldn't want you to know that you can accomplish great things, so I would do my best to keep you from meditating on that passage.

If I were your enemy, I would send people to irritate you and create distractions whenever you are about to do what God has told you to do. I would make you feel guilty when you try to work on improving yourself. This way, you will remain undisciplined and never stay focused long enough to reach your goals. I would like that because nothing of great magnitude would ever get done, and then you can get angry with God about it, or perhaps place the blame on others. I would never want you to read Proverbs 4:25-27 and Hebrews 12:1-2 because I would benefit from your distractions!

If I were your enemy, I would also make you feel guilty about things you had no control over. I would do my best to plague you with guilt so that you could never fully experience living life to the fullest. I would never want you to read John 8:44 because your eyes would be open, and you would realize I am the father of lies and there is no truth in me. This way, you would rob yourself of using the creativity God gave you, by being so guilt-ridden that you would limit yourself. I would like that because time waits for no one, and I wouldn't want you to accomplish great things in life if you read James 1:12 and decided to persevere.

If I were your enemy, I would make you blame God for every hardship and every painful season that has happened in your life, and I would make you question His very existence during the times you felt abandoned or lonely. I would keep the entire story of Joseph, found in the book of Genesis 37-45, far away from you because I wouldn't want you seeing an example of the favor and blessings of God in the midst of great suffering and difficult trials. And I certainly wouldn't want you to read Deuteronomy 31:6 or

If I Were Your Enemy!

Hebrews 12:7-11 because you would have victory over me if you realized God has not forsaken you and His plan is still at work in your life.

If I were your enemy, I would try to convince you that the Holy Spirit doesn't speak or intercede for anyone. I would keep you on social media and keep you tied to your phone, the television, radio, and just about anything that would deter you from hearing what the Holy Spirit is trying to tell you. I would never show you John 14:26 or Romans 8:26-27 because you would be too powerful if you sit long enough to hear what God has to say. So this would be one of my biggest priorities... keeping you too busy to listen!

If I were your enemy, I would work through your closest family members and cause divisions so that you will have unnecessary havoc in your life. This way, you won't be at peace in your own household, and you won't seek your secret place to pray and bring God into the atmosphere. I would love that because everyone would remain divided and that would give me a better chance of reaching every family member! I wouldn't want you all being unified, because if you started loving each other and praying together, I would have no hold on anyone. Therefore, I would encourage you to join the divisive family drama so that I could celebrate with you. And by no means would I ever want you to read Matthew 12:25!

If I were your enemy, I would tell you that you have messed up too many times for God to love you or bless you. This way, you won't even bother trying to make significant improvements in your life. And I would definitely keep you from reading Psalm 145:8-9 and Romans 3:23, because I wouldn't want you to know that the Lord is gracious and compassionate and everyone falls short and messes up at times. I would also keep you far away from learning about "The Parable of the Lost Son" [The Prodigal Son] in Luke 15:11-32, who messed up, but returned to his father,

necessary.

who welcomed him with open arms. I wouldn't want you knowing that story at all.

If I were your enemy, I would send you setback after setback so that instead of persevering and developing wisdom and character, you would get angry, discouraged, and quit before your breakthrough. This would be a huge accomplishment because I wouldn't want you knowing that God was simply trying to strengthen and mature you for greater glory. So I would definitely discourage you from reading James 1:2-4 to keep you from figuring that out.

If I were your enemy, I would try to prevent you from praising God by keeping you so busy throughout your day that you are too tired to sing praises to Him. He responds to praise and worship, and I wouldn't want Him to hear any praises coming from you! I would always hide Psalm 147:1 from you so that you will never know it is good to sing praises to God.

If I were your enemy, I would tell you that God doesn't hear your prayers, and I would try to convince you that you were wasting your time when you pray. I would never show you Ephesians 6:18 and Daniel 10:12-14, because I wouldn't want you knowing that God heard you the first time, but I am fighting against you in the spirit to try to keep you from receiving what God has to say.

If I were your enemy, I would encourage discord in your relationships so that they will never thrive. I would align you with unhealthy relationships that drain you, and try to convince you that you need them. I wouldn't want you to realize that you have the power to walk away, and stand alone with God. I would discourage you from ever reading Proverbs 31:25 to keep you from realizing that you are clothed with strength and have the power to laugh at the days to come.

If I were your enemy, I would make you focus on what you lack. I would encourage you to avoid going all in on anything God has told you to do. That way, you won't ever realize that God makes provisions along the way, as you walk in His purpose. So I would keep your attention on your bank account or your perceived lack of resources and talents, instead of reading Philippians 4:19 and walking in faith. And I would certainly hope that you never read Matthew 6:25-34 or 2 Kings 4:1-7 because you would stop worrying and begin to make bold moves that would diminish my influence over your future.

If I were your enemy, I would tell you the Bible is too complicated and I would try to convince you to never pick it up or read it, so that you can limit your knowledge of the power that dwells in you. That would be very helpful to me because I could distort just about everything you go through in life. The less you know about the words of God, the less victories you would have over me. And there is no way I would want you to read 1 Timothy 4:16 and Ephesians 6:17 because I wouldn't want you to grow in your knowledge of God. Picking up the sword of the Spirit, which is the word of God, would make you too powerful for me to stop you from helping others and achieving anything you set your mind to do!

If I were your enemy, I would throw flaming arrows at you and work even harder to get you to stop yourself, especially when you are close to your breakthrough. And I would do everything possible to keep you from reading Ephesians 6:10-20 and Isaiah 40:29-31, which would show you how to extinguish my flaming arrows and remind you that God strengthens the weary and increases the power of the weak. I would take delight in seeing you work so hard... only to quit just before the finish line.

If I were your enemy, I would keep you tired and exhausted from putting out fires that don't even belong to you. I would keep you involved with everyone else's drama and make sure they call you first so that you can feel needed and, ultimately, so that you can stay off course. I couldn't let you have too much time alone,

necessary.

thinking and planning, because you would accomplish great things, and I wouldn't want that to happen. I would never want you to understand Galatians 6:5, because I would want you to always carry loads that don't belong to you!

If I were your enemy, I would keep you engaged in deceit and fruitless conversations so that you wouldn't have time to engage in spiritual discussions and draw nearer to God. I would make sure you are the first to get the gossip calls and the first to learn about the latest entertainment news. This way, you won't remember Ephesians 4:29, Proverbs 4:24, or Proverbs 16:28 and instead of building others up, you will assist me by tearing others down and ruining relationships. I would like that because it will keep you from accessing higher spiritual realms in the presence of God where you will gain greater power over me!

If I were your enemy, I would keep you preoccupied with your image, your house, your car, and luxuries that you can't take with you when you leave this world, so that you will always be more concerned with how others view you, than with developing a close relationship with God. I would take great delight in seeing you spend your entire life centered around yourself, and it would bring great joy to me to see you compare yourself to others about things that won't last. That would make me very happy! I wouldn't want you to be aware of Psalm 49:17, because I would want you to think your items will last forever. And I certainly would never show you the passage that states, "For what shall it profit a man, if he shall gain the whole world, and lose his own soul?" (Mark 8:36 KJV). I would keep that passage far away from you!

If I were your enemy, I would do my best to keep you from exercising any self-control over your temper, over your sinful desires, over your spending, harmful behaviors, and so on. I would taunt you with pride so that you are too arrogant or too embarrassed to seek help, and I would never want you to read

If I Were Your Enemy!

Proverbs 29:1, Proverbs 29:11, Galatians 5:19-23, 1 Corinthians 10:13, 2 Timothy 4:18, and Psalm 91:14-15. This way, you would avoid repenting, and you won't realize the Lord is able to rescue you from my attacks. I would really like that because I wouldn't want you knowing that God welcomes you with open arms when you turn to Him.

If I were your enemy, I would always give you a reason to keep you from fellowshipping with any believers in the faith. I would tell you they are all fake and they just want to judge you. I would not want you to know the benefit of meeting together as stated in Hebrews 10:25, nor would I want you to realize, "As iron sharpens iron, so one person sharpens another" (Proverbs 27:17 NASB). I would want you to be dull and avoid fellowship of any kind, so that no one can help sharpen you or encourage you. And I would certainly never lead you to read Proverbs 14:12. This way, you will rely completely on your own knowledge, which works to my advantage. I would absolutely love that!

These are the things I would do... if I were your enemy!

Reflection:

I wrote nearly everything I could think of that happened throughout my life when the enemy tried to stop me from moving forward, and from writing this book. This chapter is not meant to scare you, but to open your eyes to the possibilities of what can be happening in the spiritual realm.

I pray a fire is lit inside of you to think differently. To fight differently. And to open your spiritual eyes to see if the enemy is at work in any area of your life to keep you from growing closer to God and becoming the best version of yourself.

necessary.

Recommended Reading:

- *Satan himself masquerades as an angel of light* (2 Corinthians 11:14 NIV).
- *Put on the full armor of God, so that you can take your stand against the devil's schemes. For our struggle is not against flesh and blood, but against the rulers, against the authorities, against the powers of this dark world and against the spiritual forces of evil in the heavenly realms* (Ephesians 6:11-12 NIV).
- *He was a murderer from the beginning, and does not stand in the truth because there is no truth in him. Whenever he tells a lie, he speaks from his own nature, because he is a liar and the father of lies* (John 8:44 NASB).
- *Resist the devil, and he will flee from you* (James 4:7 KJV).

Assignment:

1. Can you identify any lies the enemy has been trying to feed you?

2. How do you plan on fighting against the great deceiver when he comes against you?

3. What scripture(s) are you willing to write on the tablet of your heart so that you are always prepared to defeat his lies?

Chapter 22

Affirmation – When God Says No!

Even when your answer is no
You are still my God.

When situations don't work out the way I hope for
I will still put my trust in you.

Just hold me close
So that I can feel your presence.

Hold me close Dear God
So that I know you are near me.

When my faith is being challenged
And my heart is in despair
Please intercede for me.
And never let me go.

You are God in my good times
And God in my bad times.

Nothing shall ever take your place!

[Audio/Video version of this book is available at ZenjaGlass.com]

Chapter 22
When God Says No!

What happens when God says, "No"? Can He still be your God?

Can He still be your God when you didn't get what you wanted? Can He still be your God when life didn't turn out the way you expected? Will you still call on Him when your heart has been broken? Or is He your God only during the good seasons?

I ask you these questions because I had to ask myself these same questions when I was facing some of the greatest storms of my life. I had to decide if He would only be God of my life in my good seasons, or would He remain my God when I was in the fires and didn't feel His presence at all.

There were times in my life when I cried out to God day and night, and heard nothing. After hours and hours of pleading for a word from Him, He said absolutely nothing! I recall two specific prayers that triumphed over all the others. I prayed and prayed and prayed from the depth of my soul for God to step in, change the situations, and answer yes. Day after day, week after week, month after month, and year after year, I laid my prayer requests before God, and He still said no.

How can a loving God say no, when it's so easy to say yes?

How can my only God withhold from me what I cried out for, day and night?

I pleaded with Him to show up and change my circumstances, to heal my child, and to fix other areas of my life that seemed to be falling apart, but they remained unchanged. I praised

necessary.

and worshipped God in song and prayer, but in return, He didn't change His answer. He still said, "No."

I waited patiently for years for God to show up and change my circumstances, but instead, He insisted on just changing me!

Why would He focus on molding me when my circumstances are what needed to change? Why couldn't He just say yes? Of all the yeses He'd given in the past, why couldn't He say yes to what mattered most to me?

So I pondered the questions: *Where is God?* And, most importantly, *Can He still be my God?*

I recall the story of the apostle Paul who cried out to God to remove a painful thorn from his side, but God said no. Paul said, "To keep me from becoming conceited I was given a thorn in my flesh, a messenger of Satan, to torment me. Three times I pleaded with the Lord to take it away from me. But he said to me, 'My grace is sufficient for you, for my power is made perfect in weakness" (2 Corinthians 12:7-9 NIV).

I recall the story of Jesus, just before going to the cross, saying, "Father, if thou be willing, remove this cup from me: nevertheless not my will, but thine, be done" (Luke 22:42 KJV). God allowed the scriptures to be fulfilled, and Jesus still went to the cross.

I recall Moses doing everything he could to make God choose someone else to lead his people out of Egypt, but God said no. Moses said to the Lord, "Please, Lord, I have never been eloquent, neither recently nor in time past, nor since You have spoken to Your servant; for I am slow of speech and slow of tongue" (Exodus 4:10 NASB). God still did not change His mind about appointing Moses to do what he was commanded to do.

When God Says No!

Sometimes, God says no. Period.

Can we change His heart? Yes... if it is His will. I believe in the power of prayer and intercession, and I know that we are able to move the heart of God. But sometimes, God says no.

So, I ask the question again: Can He still be your God if His answer is no?

I wish I could lie to you and tell you that you will always receive every single thing you wish for, and you will never experience any disappointments, trials or hardships in your entire life. After all, in Matthew 7:7-8, the Bible teaches us that if we ask, we shall receive... right? Jesus also taught us that our "Father which is in heaven [gives] good things to them that ask Him" (Matthew 7:11 KJV). But we tend to forget, "not my will, but thine, be done" (Luke 22:42 KJV). That's the part that brings me to my knees. And I won't pretend as if I have all the answers. I am still a work in progress. I am still growing in my faith. I am still learning to trust in my Father, even when His answer is no.

I am moved by the words of King Solomon when he said, "Consider what God has done: Who can straighten what he has made crooked? When times are good, be happy; but when times are bad, consider this: God has made the one as well as the other" (Ecclesiastes 7:13-14 NIV).

This brings great joy and tears to my eyes because when I pray to God, I remind Him that I have no other gods to run to. He is my Alpha and my Omega, the Beginning and the End (Revelation 21:6), "who is and who was and who is to come, the Almighty" (Revelation 1:8 ESV).

necessary.

Job taught us a valuable, spiritual lesson that I pray we never forget. After all his suffering, losing dear family members, and his finances coming to a ruin, while his friends, and even his own wife, unfairly treated him, he said concerning the Lord, "Though he slay me, yet will I trust in him" (Job 13:15 KJV). Before we conclude on Job, we must also know that he kept a very real, honest, expressive relationship with God. He never cursed God, but he certainly got discouraged and angry for several chapters because he could not understand why all those calamities were happening to him. Can anyone relate to that?

This is why I love Job! He kept it real, as some of us might say. He had a genuine, authentic relationship with God, and he didn't pretend he was happy about all that happened to him. He sincerely loved God, but he was also honest about his feelings as he went through his challenges. This is what made their relationship so intimate and secure, and I can't help but wonder what lessons we can learn from those 42 chapters of the book of Job.

In Job 10:3 (NIV), he said to God, "Does it please you to oppress me, to spurn the work of your hands?" In Job 13:3 (NIV), he said, "But I desire to speak to the Almighty and to argue my case with God." In Job 12:4 (NIV), he said, "I have become a laughingstock to my friends, though I called on God and he answered- a mere laughingstock, though righteous and blameless!" In Job 19:7 (KJV), he said to God, "Behold, I cry out of wrong, but I am not heard: I cry aloud, but there is no judgment."

Job went through a lot in those 42 chapters, and I encourage you to read it all when you have time. He also did not get the best advice from his friends, who basically accused him of doing something wrong to deserve that kind of punishment from God. The Lord was later angry with those friends for giving unwise counsel, but Job prayed for them and they were forgiven in Job 42:7-9.

As a side note, when we experience difficult seasons in our lives, it does not always mean we did something wrong, or didn't pray hard enough, and so on. Be careful who you seek advice from in turbulent times. Please be wise, seek godly counsel (Proverbs 19:20), and "believe not every spirit, but try the spirits whether they are of God" (1 John 4:1 KJV).

The bottom line is, God said no to Job for nearly 42 chapters! And all along, God had a plan. A grand plan that no one could see at the time. He blessed Job's life in ways he couldn't imagine (Job 42:10-17), and while I don't wish his story on anyone, it gives me hope to trust and know that even when God says no, I must submit to His will and trust that God knows what He is doing.

For those of you who are going through difficult trials right now, please know that God is present. I know it may not look like it right now, because the pain is so deep and the situation may seem almost unbearable at times. Not only have I been there, I am there as I type these words.

I am hurting with you. I cry with you. I hope with you. I pray with you. And as one who is dealing with the greatest pain in my life right now, I also plead with you to join hands with me in the Spirit, as we lift our praises to God!

With tears forming in our eyes, we still give Him the glory. We still run to Him. He is all we have, and He must remain our God... even when His answer is no.

I ask you the question one last time: Can He still be your God?

necessary.

My answer, with tears in my eyes, is a resounding YES! My answer is yes from the depth of my soul!

He is still my God... even when He says no!

Reflection:
This was a very difficult chapter to write, and I don't have too much to say right now because I am filled with emotions. I pray that somehow, you have been inspired to keep holding on to God's unchanging hands, and you never let Him go.

Perhaps when you read the next chapter – Chapter 23, the chapter I have been avoiding to write – it will clarify things. I truly love you all.

Recommended Reading:

I encourage you to read Luke 22-24. It details the story of Jesus Christ from the time Judas betrayed Him, to the Resurrection, and His appearing again before the disciples. Pay careful attention to His prayer on the Mount of Olives before being arrested.

I also encourage you to take the time to pace yourself to read the entire book of Job. From my personal experience, his life has helped me to authentically communicate with God, and I pray it has the same impact on you.

Assignment:

1. What have you learned from the story of Jesus in Luke 22-24?

2. Are you willing to surrender to the will of God in your life? List the areas that would be challenging to fully surrender to God. If you are willing, imitate Job, and have an authentic conversation with God about this.

[Audio/Video version of this book is available at ZenjaGlass.com]

Chapter 23

Affirmation – Chapter Twenty-Three

I thought we had more time.

I thought I would see my loved one again.

No one told me the story was about to end.

I thought there would be more chapters to write.

I thought we would have more laughs.

I thought we would create more memories together.

And now, I must go on...

I must honor the loss of my loved one

By growing through the pain.

By continuing to live. To thrive. To love.

I must go on...

Until we meet again.

[Audio/Video version of this book is available at ZenjaGlass.com]

Chapter 23

Chapter Twenty-Three

How do I even begin to write the end?

How do I possibly write about the unexpected death of my son, who did not survive his stem cell transplant to combat his sickle cell disease?

He fought so hard to live. He was only twenty-three years old. He was only 23.

I don't know how to write this chapter because I feel his presence everywhere. It's as if I expect to turn the corner and see my son standing there, telling me that it was all just a bad dream. I can't count the times I replayed our last conversation; with no indication I would never see him again.

How can it be possible for someone you love so dearly to all of a sudden vanish from your life? How could God let that happen? Did He not hear my fervent prayers?

Words can't explain how it feels to lose a part of you. I've lost many loved ones before, but this is a pain that hurts my soul to its core. It's a pain that takes my breath away, and at times I have to remind myself to breathe again.

He is gone now. He is resting. Waiting for the day we shall meet again.

I can't write much more. My eyes are filled with tears, and I can barely see the keys as I type these words.

necessary.

When my son took his last breath, as my husband and I were by his side, I was playing a song in the background called, "Yes," by Shekinah Glory Ministry. It is one of the most beautiful, heartfelt songs I have ever heard in my life. It is about saying yes to the will of God over our lives. I sang and cried that song aloud to God, in the presence of all the doctors, nurses, and ministers in the room.

Even in my greatest sorrow, my answer to God was still... YES.

Yes! I will still follow you Dear Lord!

Before I end this chapter, I would like to take you on a personal journey that I experienced in the Spirit, just a few weeks after my son passed away.

Everything you are about to read is exactly what I felt, and the vision is exactly what God showed me when He visited me in the Spirit as I sat in a dark corner. This is a very personal revelation that I have not shared with others, but I feel compelled to express it at this time. I sincerely pray it encourages those who are brokenhearted, and it gives hope to those who are crushed in spirit.

***

My Vision I Saw in the Spirit, a Few Weeks After the Death of my Son:

I didn't want God to touch me.

I wanted to be angry with Him.

I wanted God to leave me in the new dark corner I built for myself to call home. I was comfortable in that tiny spot because the world was shut out, and I was alone with my new best friends, Pain and Grief.

Chapter Twenty-Three

But He would not leave me alone.

He kept standing there with His arms extended, prompting me to take hold of His hand.

I turned my back to Him because He hurt me. He hurt me by not answering my prayers with a Yes.

I still loved Him, but I didn't want Him to touch me, or ask me to do anything for that matter.

He refused my prayers. He answered NO to my request to let my son live.

So... I sat in my corner... with my back turned away from His invitation.

But He would not leave me alone...

I felt as if God was on one side of the room, and I was in the same room, but on the other side of the wall. I had no energy to read my Bible. I couldn't even pray. I don't even know if I wanted to pray. I could only moan hums of sorrow and grief.

I remember thinking, "My answer is still YES to you Lord. I don't have any other gods to turn to. You are the only living God in my life, but haven't I been through enough long suffering? Was my praise and worship not enough? Why did you allow my son to die? He only wanted to live."

Night after night, I cried myself to sleep. Each morning, I was hoping to see my son standing in front of me, telling me I had a bad dream, and he was fine. That morning never arrived.

So... I continued to sit in my corner... with my back turned away from His invitation.

necessary.

But He would not leave me alone…

He did not turn away.

He stood there waiting patiently for me. Arms extended. Gentle. Patient. Kind. Loving. Present.

I was too weak to pray, so I asked for assistance. I asked the Holy Spirit to pray for me with words that I could not express. I cried, and moaned, and groaned, as He interceded, and prayed for me.

I don't know what He said, but I believe my prayers were heard because I began to feel my Father gently lifting me up and embracing me. I did not hug Him back. I was too weak to hold Him, and to be quite honest, I didn't want to hold Him. But I was glad He held me.

He wasn't dismayed by my lack of embrace. He acted as if nothing happened… as if, He knew who I was becoming. He gently wrapped my limp arms around Him and upheld my embrace as He listened to my loud cries of agony, until I could cry no more. Then, He took me by the hand and began to lead me down a path.

"Jesus, where are you taking me?"

He said nothing.

So, we just walked. Quietly.

He began to walk me through the seasons of my life. Every major trial and difficult season I had ever experienced appeared before my eyes. It was as if I were the main character in an adventure movie, directed by God. I stood in His theater as He played each season of my life, allowing me

Chapter Twenty-Three

the time to visit my past dark corners and observe how He provided a way for me to stand.

As I observed my life play out before my eyes, I noticed how I began to change from season to season. Something was different about my appearance. In each new scene, I seemed to be clothed with more strength and dignity. Something was different about the way I held my head just a little higher as I walked into each new season of my life.

I seemed wiser in the way I handled situations. I appeared more courageous than before, and I seemed to grow in my perseverance. In each season that followed, a stronger character started to emerge. Despite all the opposition I endured, I looked more hopeful and, dare I say, faithful, as I fought my battles. It was as if each season had a purpose to equip me for the next one. It was as if each season was… necessary.

I also noticed that I wasn't in any season by myself. While I did not always feel God's presence, He was there all along. Through it all, He stood there waiting patiently for me. Arms extended. Gentle. Patient. Kind. Loving.

Then, the Lord did something I did not expect. He took me by the shoulders and turned me around to see who was also watching my seasons. I had no idea the room was filled with spectators!

They were all watching me.

They seemed to be observing me from their dark corners.

I looked to the Lord with a bit of confusion on my face because I did not understand why a crowd was watching my seasons.

necessary.

I did not understand why they were all standing there, like lost sheep, looking for us to help them.

He said nothing.

I stood there for a moment. Then I said:

"But God, I have nothing to give them. I am tired. I am weak. I am barely hanging on myself. I have been through so much and fought through so many seasons of long-suffering. Why would You ask me to help others when I am fighting to have a relationship with You? How can I possibly help them when I am in a season of sorrow? I love You God, and my answer is still Yes to Your will for my life. And though You have allowed me to be slayed in this season, I still put my trust in You. But how am I able to help anyone, when You are my only hope and strength, and all I have to offer is my pain and suffering, and my will to stay in the fight and cling to You?"

The more I spoke those words, the more my spectators began to walk out of their dark places. It was almost as if they were somehow attracted to the light they saw in us. And somehow, the closer they walked toward us, the brighter they started to shine!

I turned to the Lord once again, because I did not understand how He could use such a broken vessel to help others.

I asked Him one last question. I said, "God, how is it possible that in my darkest season, I am able to help them shine brighter?"

He said nothing.

He only smiled.

Chapter Twenty-Three

Reflection:

I don't know what to say. I am still reflecting as I type these words. I am still fighting the good fight and doing my best to honor God in my life, even though my heart aches, and I miss my son from the depth of my soul.

I can only say that Jesus is still Lord of my life, and I am willing to be used by Him to encourage others to never give up on His unfailing love.

If you can identify with my story, I pray with all my heart that God gives you the strength to come out of your dark corner and allow Him to embrace you.

Just let Him hold you... as He is now holding me.

And even if you don't have the strength to embrace Him, just let Him hold you.

I sincerely love you all.

Z.

Recommended Reading:

Read the entire book of John to learn about the life and character of Jesus Christ. I am recommending this book of the Bible because it helped me develop a deeper relationship with God. I pray it has the same impact in your life.

necessary.

Assignment:

I do not have an assignment for you; I have a request. Please take some time to pray; not only for yourselves, but also for all those who are brokenhearted. In fact, I encourage you to take it a step farther and write a prayer list consisting of those you will pray for each day this week.

People all over the world are hurting in so many ways, and these are the days we need to be committed to praying at all times, on all occasions.

Chapter 24

Affirmation – A Letter to the Enemy - Part 2

God has captured the ancient serpent
And crushed him with His mighty power!

We shall no longer fear him!
We shall triumph as Priests and Kings!

We are heirs of God!
We walk in power and authority!

We did not receive a Spirit that makes us a slave to fear!
We were given a Spirit of sonship!
We are heirs of the Almighty God!

The ancient serpent has been captured!
He shall NEVER rise again!

[Audio/Video version of this book is available at ZenjaGlass.com]

Chapter 24

A Letter to the Enemy - Part 2

You. Have. Lost!

God. Has. Won!

All this time, I thought you were attacking me. I never knew you were attacking what was inside of me. All this time, I thought I was your primary aim. I thought that's why you attacked me so many times, and made every effort to discourage me from moving forward. But now my eyes have been opened. Now I realize... I was never the real target!

The real target was against the light you saw inside of me. The real target was against the mission of the light. The real target was against God!

You know that your time here is short (Revelation 12:12). You tried your best to convince me to walk away from God, because you saw something in me that I didn't see in myself. You saw more than my physical body. You saw the nations He predestined to reach through me (Ephesians 1:5). You saw who I was becoming. All along, you wanted me to denounce God, abandon my faith, and turn away from the purpose I was predestined to fulfill. Now it all makes sense. That's why you hate me so much!

I feared you for many years. I guess I just didn't know any better. I didn't know the power inside of me was far greater than you (1 John 4:4) and I certainly didn't understand the

necessary.

dominion I was given (Genesis 1:26, Psalm 8:4-8), the position as a priest and king (Revelation 1:6, Revelation 5:10, 1 Peter 2:9-10) and the level of ranking as an heir of God, and joint-heir with Christ (Romans 8:17) that was placed over my life.

You waited patiently to sneak upon me like a roaring lion during my weakest moments in life (1 Peter 5:8). You masqueraded as an angel of light (2 Corinthians 11:14), and during the months following my son's death, I did not know you were that close to me. You crawled so well on your belly, filled with poison and death certificates! You stared me straight in the eyes and fed me an illusion as you slithered closer and closer, filling my heart with guilt, grief, and despair, robbing me of purpose, beating me with wrongful convictions, and seducing me into dark chambers with your lies and deceit!

You did your best to make me believe that somehow I failed in life. That somehow I failed as a mother by not preventing my son's death. You whispered to me over and over again, "What if you'd gotten your son to the hospital sooner? What if you asked more questions about his medications? What if you searched for alternative treatments sooner than later? Would he still be alive?"

You were so skilled and so convincing, that despite the obvious fact that I did everything a parent could have possibly done to save her child, I listened to you and contemplated if perhaps you were right. I felt myself sinking deeper and deeper into guilt and grief, to the point where I was too weak to even pray.

You had my head spinning with so many regrets and feelings of guilt, that I couldn't even see you moving closer and closer to me. I wasn't paying attention as you began to coil around my body. I didn't know how tightly you were constricting me by feeding me "what ifs" and pulling me away from the calling God has on my life.

But you didn't seem to learn from the previous time you left me on my knees in the presence of my Father. Somehow you keep miscalculating the power that is manifested when I am prostrated before my God. I stayed on my knees and begged God to rescue me. I sat in His presence as often as I could for months, pleading for Him to make His presence known, and to deliver me from your lies and deceit.

I stayed in the secret place, deep within, where Christ dwells (Romans 8:11, Psalm 91:1); the place of hidden treasures filled with wisdom and knowledge (Colossians 2:2-3), and I found truth. I found peace. I found my purpose in the pain.

You are a liar! The father of lies. And when you lie, you speak your native tongue (John 8:44)!

As God began to comfort me and open my eyes, I saw you for who you truly are… a cunning serpent, skilled in deceit, selfishly clever, and filled with fury because you know your time is short!

You are a liar! You are an accuser. Your name bears no truth. And I will no longer answer to your call!

Every flaming arrow you sent my way has now been returned to you! My momma taught me how to praise God in my storms. Now, I will praise Him all the more! You have lost the battle to defeat me. I will show your scars to the nations so that they may be encouraged and inspired to turn away from your deception and seek the presence of God.

I will use every affliction you sent my way to convince others to come out of their dark places and trust in the love of God.

necessary.

I will use every setback and every obstacle you placed in my path to teach others how to overcome them as they pursue their dreams in life. I will turn all my pain into gold, by teaching others how to seek God first when they are tempted to give up. And I will write about every tear I've shed so that others can find a reason to smile as they turn to God!

Everything you meant for evil has turned out for my good, and the good of my Father (Isaiah 54:17)!

And by the way... I am just getting started!

So, thank you once again for playing your role. Thank you for all the thorns you placed in my paths. Your evil intentions have only pushed me closer to God. And the closer I get to Him, the more I become His reflection. The more I reflect His image, the more nations are drawn to the light they see in me! And the more the nations are drawn to the light, the more they become God's reflection.

When you attacked me, you attacked my Father. Somehow you must have forgotten; He has NEVER lost a battle...and He never will!

You can no longer hurt me!

I am already dead.

Dead to myself.

Alive in Christ!

A Letter to the Enemy – Part 2

Reflection:

I visited my son's gravesite before writing this chapter today. I needed to be reminded that life is short (James 4:14).

God has kept us here for a divine purpose, and we must let Him use us for His glory.

Before I left the cemetery, I whispered into his gravesite, "Son, momma has to go now. While momma is still above ground, momma has work to do. I gotta go help other people who are hurting to find hope in God."

To God be all the glory.

I love you all.

Z.

Recommended Reading:

- *The reason the Son of God appeared was to destroy the works of the devil* (1 John 3:8 ESV).
- *For he who is in you is greater than he who is in the world* (1 John 4:4 ESV).
- *Then war broke out in heaven. Michael and his angels fought against the dragon, and the dragon and his angels fought back. But he was not strong enough, and they lost their place in heaven. The great dragon was hurled down- that ancient serpent called the devil, or Satan, who leads the whole world astray. He was hurled to the earth, and his angels with him ...*

necessary.

> *They triumphed over him by the blood of the Lamb and by the word of their testimony* (Revelation 12:7-11 NIV).
> - *He is filled with fury, because he knows that his time is short* (Revelation 12:12 NIV).
> - *No weapon that is formed against thee shall prosper; and every tongue that shall rise against thee in judgment thou shalt condemn* (Isaiah 54:17 KJV).
> - *For death is the destiny of everyone; the living should take this to heart* (Ecclesiastes 7:2 NIV).
> - *And Jesus came and spake unto them, saying, All power is given unto me in heaven and in earth. Go ye therefore, and teach all nations, baptizing them in the name of the Father, and of the Son, and of the Holy Ghost: Teaching them to observe all things whatsoever I have commanded you: and, lo, I am with you always, even unto the end of the world. Amen* (Matthew 28:18-20 KJV).

Assignment:

1. How do these passages impact the way you view the enemy (Satan)?

2. In your own words, describe the power of God. Use at least one scripture. Be specific about the power God has over Satan and the power God has made available for you.

3. What decision will you make to commit your life to God and surrender to His divine plan?

A Dedication to My Son

A Dedication to My Son

In dedication to my loving son, Jared A. Glass, momma will always love you. I pray you are proud that momma has done her best to help others come to accept the love of God.

Jared A. Glass

(December 12, 1997- April 9, 2021)

Many years ago, God woke me up in the middle of the night and told me I would write a book and it shall be called, "necessary." He even showed me exactly what the book should look like. I saw a vision of a black book, with only the word "necessary." on the front cover. I made a note of that and went back to bed. Aside from a few attempts to write some chapters, I didn't get much accomplished.

In 2021, several years later, God woke me up again in the middle of the night and told me that it was now time to start writing that book. As I sat on my bedroom floor at 3 a.m., with a lit candle, I cried like a baby as I started to write because I knew something major was about to happen. I knew God was about to change lives. But I had no idea, just a few days later, on April 9, 2021, my son would die.

I am sure by this point, based on the title of my book, you expected me to tell you that everything you have gone through in your life was necessary. But I don't think it's my place to tell you that. I can only share my life and hope that, by the grace of God, you are inspired to draw nearer to Him, despite whatever difficulties you may be experiencing.

I do not hold any ministerial titles. I am simply a woman who loves God with all her heart, and I do my best to walk in obedience to His will for my life. I pray my book has helped

A Dedication to My Son

you to unlock the greatness inside of you by changing your perspective of how you view difficult seasons in your life. And most importantly, I pray it moves you closer to knowing who you are in the sight of God.

I have learned how short and precious life truly is. In fact, I still recall the last words I said to my son on the morning of this death. I was certain I would see his face again later that day, but death does not always make announcements. In the blink of an eye, my life was forever changed.

I can't force you to accept Christianity, nor can I force you to desire a deeper relationship with God. I can only share my testimony and pray that it moves you closer to the God in heaven that I serve.

So I will end by saying: If you are willing, please make a commitment to follow God and seek the Lord while He may be found (Isaiah 55:6, Romans 10:9, Acts 2:38, John 3:16). Don't ever allow the enemy to convince you that you are not good enough. Our Father in heaven welcomes you with open arms. Please seek Him while you are still above ground... because tomorrow is promised to no one.

"For death is the destiny of everyone; the living should take this to heart" (Ecclesiastes 7:2 NIV).

I love you all.

Zenja "Z." Glass

[Audio/Video version of this book is available at ZenjaGlass.com]

AFTERWORD

Afterword

When I sit alone with God, I often imagine Him sitting next to me on a bench as we observe my life. And for some reason, I always imagine Japanese cherry blossom trees before us.

I have chosen to end my book by sharing an intimate revelation that was revealed to me in the Spirit as I sat next to Jesus and started the journey to write this book:

The Lord and I sat on a beautiful white bench, surrounded by what seemed like hundreds and hundreds of Japanese cherry blossom trees. The wind was filled with blossoms all around us. And the ground was completely covered with pink, white, and maroon cherry blossom buds.

No words were exchanged. We simply sat on a bench, in a sea of blossoms, staring straight ahead, in complete peace, surrounded by beauty, wisdom and understanding, as we watched my entire life unfold before my eyes... every season... every tear... every disappointment... every celebration... every milestone... every victory. Somehow, as He sat next to me, I realized... all was well.

All was well with my soul, in the hidden secret place, where I sat with my Father.

As I surveyed my life among the blossoms, all of it was beautiful before me. I can still feel the gentle wind and the touch of petals blowing on my face as the Japanese cherry blossom trees stood so beautifully, on opposite sides of a long pathway that led into eternity.

As we sat on the bench, He slowly took hold of my right hand and motioned for me to look down.

Afterword

What is this that I see?

I see a sea of Japanese cherry blossom petals all around me. I see roots running deep into the ground from my feet.

I see a strong tree, and solid bark as my arms and legs.

I see branches and vines filled with blossoms, extending from my body. I see blossoms everywhere!

And then it dawned on me. We are all a part of these glorious cherry blossom trees with magnificent colors and majesty!

Now it all makes perfect sense. Every season. Every color. Every spring. And every fall.

All of it is beautiful.

And dare I say... necessary.

[Audio/Video version of this book is available at ZenjaGlass.com]

ACKNOWLEDGEMENTS

[Audio/Video version of this book is available at ZenjaGlass.com]

Acknowledgements

First and foremost, I have to give thanks to God for entrusting me to write His book. It has been one of the most difficult, yet rewarding, accomplishments I have ever done, and I am grateful that God gave me the words to say to help His people.

Dear Lord, I pray you are pleased with your book. And I look forward to hearing you one day say to me: "Well done, good and faithful servant. Well done!"

I would like to give special thanks to my family, friends, and podcast subscribers for all your encouragement. You all have witnessed this book unfold in real time, and I am grateful to have you all in my life.

I must give special thanks to my editor Sharon Gauthier for taking on my project at the last minute to proofread my final copy. Sharon, you are amazing, and I am so grateful for you!

I would also like to thank Virginia Lefler and Kathy Heinen for loving me enough to invite me to your Bible sessions many years ago. The principles I learned from your classes have changed my life!

And I certainly can't end this section without acknowledging my staff members. I am blessed to have such a wonderful team! The world may never know how many times I had to lean on you all for your motivation and for your support to keep going and finish this book.

Thank you all from the bottom of my heart!

To God be all the glory!

Much love,

Zenja (Z.) Glass

[Audio/Video version of this book is available at ZenjaGlass.com]

About the Author

Zenja Glass is a business owner, motivational speaker, author, and most importantly, a woman after God's heart. She is married, has four adult children, and resides in the USA.

Her motivational podcast, *Unlocking Greatness Podcast with Zenja Glass,* streams all around the world to inspire the brokenhearted and encourage others to draw near to God as they pursue their dreams in life.

She cares deeply about helping children who are victims of human trafficking and kids with chronic medical conditions.

Her primary goal is to help people apply biblical principles in every aspect of their lives to overcome all obstacles and achieve superior results.

[Audio/Video version of this book is available at ZenjaGlass.com]

The Lord's Prayer

Our Father which art in heaven,

Hallowed be thy name.

Thy kingdom come,

Thy will be done in earth, as it is in heaven.

Give us this day our daily bread.

And forgive us our debts, as we forgive our debtors.

And lead us not into temptation, but deliver us from evil:

For thine is the kingdom, and the power, and the glory,

for ever.

Amen.

Matthew 6:9-13 (KJV)

[Audio/Video version of this book is available at ZenjaGlass.com]

The Lord is My Shepherd

The Lord is my shepherd; I shall not want.

He maketh me to lie down in green pastures: he leadeth me beside the still waters.

He restoreth my soul: he leadeth me in the paths

of righteousness for his name's sake.

Yea, though I walk through the valley of the shadow of death, I will fear no evil:

for thou art with me; thy

rod and thy staff they comfort me.

Thou preparest a table before me

in the presence of mine enemies:

thou anointest my head with oil; my cup runneth over.

Surely goodness and mercy shall follow me

all the days of my life:

and I will dwell in the house of the Lord for ever.

Psalm 23 (KJV)

[Audio/Video version of this book is available at ZenjaGlass.com]

Thank you for taking the time to read my book.

I sincerely pray you have been encouraged.

Please take a moment to write a book review and share what you have learned with others.

If you post a social media review, please tag me so that I can personally thank you.

To learn more about my latest releases, access the audio/video version of this book, or inquire about additional services, please visit:

www.ZenjaGlass.com

[Audio/Video version of this book is available at ZenjaGlass.com]

Please use this section to take additional notes and write prayers as you reflect on all God has done for you.

Notes:

_____
_____
_____
_____
_____
_____
_____
_____
_____
_____
_____
_____
_____

Prayers:

Made in United States
Orlando, FL
10 April 2023